Tell Them About Me

A Journey Through Bipolar Disorder
and the
Faith Walk into Remission

A Christian Testimony and Memoir

by Maria Eva Jacobs

iwarble publishing

Tell Them About Me: A Journey Through Bipolar Disorder and the Faith Walk into Remission, Copyright ©2025 by Maria Eva Jacobs. All rights reserved.

Printed in the United States of America. No part of this book may be used or reproduced, in any manner, performed or copied in any form without written permission except in the case of brief quotations embodied in critical articles and reviews.

For information or additional copies, contact:
tellthemaboutmeauthor@gmail.com
iwarble publishing

Cover art created by Adam Rice Creative
Author photo credit Christin Da'Shawn Harris

ISBN: 979-8-218-82539-3

First Edition, 2025
10 9 8 7 6 5 4 3 2 1

Dedication

This book is lovingly dedicated to my late mother
and father, Mike and Jan Jacobs, whose
faith and unconditional love made it all possible.

Acknowledgments

First and foremost, I thank my Lord and Savior Jesus Christ, who met me in my darkest hour and turned my brokenness into beauty. Without Him, this book and my life would not exist in the way that it does today. May both be a testimony to His grace and mercy.

To my late mother and father, Mike and Jan Jacobs, to whom this book is dedicated. Thank you for your unconditional love, your unending prayers, and your unwavering faith. You stood with me when I could not stand on my own. You believed in God's promises, even when I couldn't see them for myself. Your faith and strength in the Lord have been an example that will be with me for the rest of my days.

To my sister and brothers, extended family, dear friends, and brothers and sisters in Christ, thank you for your encouragement, support, patience, and presence in my life, and most especially for your prayers. God made you all part of my journey for a reason, a glorious reason! The mountain was tough to climb, but your love lifted me and made it possible to persevere and emerge stronger on the other side.

To my faith family at St. Elias Church and St. Mary's Hudson. Thank you for your prayers and for the privilege of serving through music. Both have deepened my walk with Christ beyond measure.

To my editorial staff, Janice Hermsen and LeRue Press. Thank you for the care and commitment you brought to editing this book and collaborating with me to design the cover. It is because of you I'm able to share it all with the world. You honored my story.

To my advising literary agent, Joe Durepos. Thank you for taking the time to read my book and for offering your invaluable insight that it is so much more than a memoir, it is indeed a Christian testimony.

To my generous, early readers—Your truthful hearts and open minds breathed life into the early drafts of this book. Thanks you for the loving feedback you shared, which helped to shape my words.

To the music community that has embraced me, from Los Angeles to Cleveland. From my fellow musicians, producers, and engineers, to the radio stations and listeners who have supported my work over the years, thank you. Music has been a life-saving gift from God, a form of worship, and a powerful avenue for sharing my story.

Thank you to the Kent State University School of Music Hoban High School, St. Barnabas, St. Joseph Randolph and Open Tone Music. I'm grateful for the support and space you gave me to continue to grow as an artist and educator while bringing this book to life.

Finally, to everyone who reads this book, whether you too are living with bipolar disorder, or you love someone who is, thank you. It is my prayer that you find hope within these pages that chronicle not only my struggles, but also my recovery and remission. I pray that upon reading, you will know that healing is possible because no one is beyond the healing power of God's perfect and redeeming love.

Table of Contents

Acknowledgements...IV

Preface...VIII

Chapter 1
Living with Manic Depressive Illness...1

Chapter 2
Growing Up in Brooklyn, Surviving Ohio State...20

Chapter 3
On the Radio...46

Chapter 4
LA LA Land Wasn't Easy...60

Chapter 5
Chasing Dreams All The Way Home...87

Chapter 6
The Crooked Lines That Led Me Back To Faith...98

Chapter 7
God's in the Music, The Spiritual Art of Jazz Singing...116

Chapter 8
God's in the Classroom, The Spiritual Art of Teaching...137

Chapter 9
Seventy Times Seven, The Spiritual Art of Forgiveness...153

Chapter 10
"Do everything in Love," The Spiritual Art of Relationships...164

Chapter 11
Designed by God, A Life Set To Music...185

Epilogue...211

Preface

According to the National Institute of Mental Health or NIMH, there are 5.7 million people in America who are afflicted with Manic and Depressive Illness, or bipolar disorder as it later came to be known. If you are one of them, this book is for you, your family, and your friends who long to see you living a life in full remission.

I hope you will read *"Tell Them About Me"* with hope in your heart, and that you appreciate its candor and honesty. While I do use my life as an example of how full remission is possible, what you're really reading is a Christian testimony of the many ways in which Jesus can show just how far His love, grace and mercy will go. It's all so immeasurable.

The *'Me'* in *Tell Them About Me*, is Him. It's Jesus, and the testimony I share begins with the reflection on my life with this Affective Mood Disorder. It continues with Him meeting me in my darkest hour, and it ends with a profound joy and gratitude for His love beyond comprehension.

As hard as it may be to believe, I have done more with my life as a result of living with this condition than I ever could have without it. I refused to give up. That indeed, is solely by the grace of God. My drive and determination are the direct result of a struggle that ultimately led to a closer walk with Christ.

On this walk, He directed my footsteps spiritually, personally and musically. All of the difficulties I endured have revealed themselves in the gift of music designed by God. Be it Sacred or Secular, the Holy Spirit is at the center of everything I sing and write.

My life with bipolar disorder is akin to the Latin, Catholic phrase *Felix Culpa*, or *'blessed fall.'* In truth, I have fallen many times. The deeper truth is that Jesus used my *falls* to bless not only me, but also those whom my story and testimony would one day help. He used my *falls* to show me that I can do nothing without Him. Simply put, mine is a beautiful resurrection story. It is the story of a deeper conversion to the Catholic faith. Remember this when you read difficult passages.

Twenty years ago when I began writing, this book was solely about life's struggles with a debilitating disease. I wrote page after page that would chronicle a tremendous battle, the life I tried to live in between set backs, and a profound desperation to hold on to the faith that the disease eroded for years.

After months of writing and crying, I came to the conclusion that I had to put the book down for a while. Not only did I need a mental break from reliving a lot of pain, I strongly felt that I needed to live out the next few chapters of a life that had yet to experience the supernatural, healing power of God.

I put the book down for years, fully believing that the worst was behind me, and that the next chapters would be filled with triumph and victory. For a while, they were.

I received victory as a lucky infant when I was baptized into the Catholic Church, victory in Jesus! Unfortunately, a tremendous amount of pain evolved before

I was able to put Him first. Sometimes you cannot find Him until you are driven to your knees. Of course I had Him in my mind before, but it took thirty years of pain to truly put Him first in my heart every day.

***

On my journey, I did experience some church folk who did not believe that bipolar disorder and depression required medical attention. They believed it was something sent by the devil requiring only spiritual healing. Well, spiritual healing is most definitely, a key part of my story, but I would have died without medical attention. I see now there was simply no way for them to understand something they had never experienced themselves, but I felt so judged, and that was painful.

We all want to fit in and be accepted and understood, I know I did. Yet for so long, it seemed everywhere I turned there was someone to diminish the gravity of the condition, and the need for medication. In the process, they devalued me, until I devalued myself.

I can remember one day talking to a family member whose opinion I mistakenly cared too much about. I had just been fired from one of my stressful sales positions and was understandably upset. Holding down jobs while dealing with bipolar disorder was difficult to say the least, but he was less than empathetic. In a careless and crass manner, he told me I wasn't bipolar, I just needed to grow up. Ouch! That hurt.

That was just one of many examples of the insensitivity I experienced from people I loved. It was infuriating and heartbreaking at the same time. I was clearly alone in this struggle, surrounded by people who just did not understand, or even worse, simply didn't care.

***

Many people just could not see its benefits, but without medication, life would be filled with agony and fear on a daily basis. Yes, God can heal a person completely with no more need for medical treatment. There are tireless examples of this in the Bible. In my case however, He had something very different and specific in mind, something that made for a powerful testimony. I was being healed spiritually, learning to trust and praise God, even while living with a chronic illness that does indeed require medication.

I was frequently called weak for taking it. In fact, I was harassed by several groups of people in my life years ago who tried over and over again to take me off of it. It was incredibly painful and as a result, I isolated for years. There were very few people I could turn to, especially about this condition. If not for the incredible support of two lifelong friends and a supportive family, I would have ended up homeless or worse.

***

Throughout this book, you will still read about struggle, but there is so much more now. As I began to experience God's healing power, I began to write more of His immeasurable goodness, mercy and grace; none of which I deserved, but all of which I received.

Then there was His gift of music, which brings me closer to Him, which belongs to Him. It's not mine, I'm just the steward who tries relentlessly to give it back to Him every day.

I've endured bipolar disorder my entire adult life. I hope after reading this book, that will not be the only thing you will take away with you. I hope you learn to take Him with you, Jesus! I also hope that if you've ever doubted the need to medicate bipolar disorder, you will come to terms with what a blessing it is that we have such help. It would otherwise be a debilitating disease.

God makes no mistakes. I am *'fearfully and wonderfully made' (Psalm 139)* and God has led me down this difficult road for a reason. He knew the testimony I would one day be overjoyed to share. I was chosen, and so are you. If you are reading this, I hope that you will soon come to realize that you too can have a powerful testimony.

A *'blessed fall'* can bring you to an upright walk with Christ. Mine brought me to a blessed and supernatural experience with Him when I fell to rock bottom. If you'd like proof that miracles, grace and mercy do exist, keep reading. I took Jesus seriously when He said, *Tell Them About Me*!

Chapter 1
Living with Manic Depressive Illness

To live with manic and depressive illness, or bipolar disorder as it later came to be known, is to accept and even embrace the highs, lows and ugliness that will follow. Professor of psychiatry and author, Kay Redfield Jamison, expressed this and answered a deeply personal question in her memoir *"An Unquiet Mind: A Memoir of Moods and Madness.*

She asked herself if, given the choice, she would choose to have the disease. She answered in the affirmative because lithium was available to her, and it was an effective treatment in bringing about a much more manageable life. She eloquently explained that because of those highs and lows, she has felt more deeply and intensely; that she has even loved and laughed more, been more loved by others, and cried more. She wrote that she has essentially had more profound experiences than those without this potentially crippling disease.

This resonated with me. I too would choose to have it, and for the same reason: the medication works. Bipolar disorder has indeed brought with it difficulties, but also many blessings, if you can believe that. I've been enriched as a musical artist and now, celebrate a reclaimed yet even richer faith life once eroded by this disease. How could I not? After all the nastiness that I lived to write about, I finally enjoy a full life in remission, realizing and rejoicing that this healing is solely by the grace of God.

Well after all, isn't that how He works? He makes beautiful music out of a nasty mess, and my life was a nasty mess for years. It was an absolute hellacious journey, on which it often seemed God was not listening. It appeared as though the desperate prayers of a suffering soul were going unattended.

He was listening, however. The disease was a liar, among so many other maddening things that made for that nasty mess.

Bipolar disorder is relentless, inducing fear, self-doubt and self-loathing. It tried hard to separate the close, ethnic family that I belonged to, and who became caregivers through tumultuous times that made caring for me so, so tough.

They never left and they never kicked me out, no matter how the difficulties escalated with screaming, yelling at one another and slamming doors to get away from heated arguments. Despite it all, they wanted to see me overcome and achieve dreams, but the disease lied about that too, telling me they wanted to see my demise, which caused much of that fear.

Those intrusive thoughts caused mistrust that had me wanting to run away forever. Something made me stay, however. God was at work even when I didn't believe it, and the desire to overcome, was one of the many examples of His presence.

***

Early on, there were so many unanswered questions swirling through an already cluttered mind. Once lucid and moderately stable, it was necessary to become more educated about bipolar disorder.

Doctors were helpful, but more research would be imperative, beginning with the bipolar section of the *Diagnostic Statistical Manual of Mental Disorders IV*. It described in detail the symptoms and characteristics of what was becoming a raging disorder filled with suicidal ideation, depression, mania, and even both simultaneously, which doctors called mixed states. They were all present and persistent throughout the course of necessary treatment.

It is important to note that there are two types of this disease. Bipolar 1 Disorder, and the less severe Bipolar 2 Disorder. Bipolar 1 generally surfaces for the first time in the form of a major depressive episode, followed by an episode of full-blown mania. (2) It is also usually passed along genetically from the maternal side of the family. (3) Down the family tree a bit, there was a distant cousin on my mother's side who was hospitalized for manic depressive illness. This was back when there was no medication. I also swear my maternal grandmother, my Nana, was a bit bipolar. She was hypomanic at times. To my memory, I can remember that she was frequently elevated, just not to the point of full-blown manic episodes. There were many occasions when her moods did swing. She could be up and down like a roller coaster, but her spirit was unbreakable, something I like to believe she passed along to me.

Other criteria help doctors decipher between Bipolar 1 and Bipolar 2 Disorder, as their symptoms overlap. With Bipolar 1 you generally have an autoimmune disorder. (4) I had two, Hashimoto's thyroid disease and alopecia, which has now resulted in total loss of the hair on my head and body. I meet all three of these criteria, and I endure Bipolar 1 Disorder, instead of its slightly milder counterpart.

Clinical descriptions were helpful, but I needed to hear more from people who were also afflicted. Two more books were useful to that end, one of them written by Patty Duke, an actress, and the other also written by Jamison, though this one not a memoir.

Touched With Fire: Manic-Depressive Illness and the Artistic Temperament explores well-known artists who also lived with manic and depressive illness. From composers to poets, she takes us on a detailed journey of their struggles and how their creativity was affected by them.

As an artist myself, *Touched With Fire* was an important read for coming to terms with what was becoming my *new normal*. Learning to navigate through this rough terrain, brought with it a lift to a cherished artistic life as a singer and songwriter.

In *Call Me Anna* by Patty Duke, the actress left nothing out as she detailed her lifelong struggle with this condition and how much medication helped. Reading her story served well in gaining self-acceptance and validation. The disease was real, and without medication, it was real bad.

That was the other wonderful thing about Jamison and Duke's books. They both stressed the importance of medication and credited it with their ability to live a normal life. This is something everyone with bipolar disorder needs to hear. Most people afflicted, including myself, just didn't want to take it early on, before we could see its many benefits.

***

Tell Them About Me

Like Jamison, I too have loved more, felt more pain and joy, and have had a much more heightened awareness of my environment. Often, it was an environment that was not always what it appeared to be. For a long time, thoughts were broken, while tearfully peering at life through a broken filter. Still, much of what I have endured since that first episode has fueled creativity and determination to become an accomplished singer, songwriter, and author.

Though finally enjoying a rich and full faith life today, for years I could not feel the peaceful, comforting presence of the Holy Spirit. I forced myself to go to church on and off for nearly three decades, trying desperately to hold on to the faith I was raised in, but feeling nothing. Impaired most of the time and in tears throughout the Mass, I pretty much went only on Easter and Christmas like so many wayward Catholics. This was possibly the most painful part of living with bipolar disorder. The disease continued to tell more and more lies. They caused tremendous pain, that by the grace of God, I would eventually overcome.

***

The doctors say that the first major depressive episode I experienced may have been triggered by a difficult breakup in college. It's hard to tell initially, but external forces can be a trigger for someone who is chemically predisposed to such an illness as bipolar disorder.

While external sources cannot cause manic depression, they can trigger episodes. Mania, for example, tends to rear its ugly head in the spring when the light and the season changes, just as depression emerges in the winter for the same reason. Too much stress in one's life and not being compliant with medication can cause a bipolar episode, and so can an intense emotional situation like a bad breakup, which I experienced early on.

    The condition was not a simple one. Enduring more than the mood swings, there was also intense fear, paranoia, reality testing issues and persecutory delusions, or the belief that everyone wanted to hurt me and obstruct my goals. There were times the paranoia was so profound, I would barricade myself in the bedroom, believing I was literally under surveillance. I was afraid to change my clothes for fear someone was watching, I used to go into my closet to undress. It was Orwellian. Big brother was always watching. Thoughts raced so much that I lost about twenty pounds during a two-week-long, manic period.

    This paranoia, this thought disorder, made it difficult for the doctors to treat me initially. It was a bit of a dual diagnosis which also included schizophrenic-like symptoms. This is was very typical of bipolar disorder.

    In 1990, at the initial onset of the disease, I used to drive around in Cleveland at night believing there were people somewhere waiting for me. I was convinced there was some kind of network of people following me, communicating through license plates and freeway signs. I also thought construction was purposely put there to keep me from my destination.

    One night as I drove by an empty baseball park on the east side of Cleveland, I saw the lights on and mistakenly believed it was a sign that people were waiting for me. I pulled into the parking lot, which was dark. There were young people standing around, drinking and partying. I sat alone in my car with the radio on as if I were waiting for instructions. After about a half an hour, I finally realized I didn't belong and left. Everything was surreal. I believed things that were not real, and I disbelieved things that were really happening.

When a close family member died suddenly, I started laughing. My family was visibly shaken and upset but I was convinced it was all a joke, and that they were intentionally playing tricks on me. I can remember sitting and waiting by the phone one afternoon while home alone, waiting for him to call and tell me, "Just kidding honey, I'm alive!" It was not until I saw him lying in his coffin at the wake that I was finally convinced of his death. My, how tremendously disturbing this all was.

If these experiences remind you at all of the film "*A Beautiful Mind*", just remember, that film came years later in 2001. You're right though, Ron Howard and Russell Crowe did a brilliant job of depicting the schizophrenic episodes of one John Nash, mathematician. Before I was properly medicated, I experienced similar episodes.

Following this desperate place, but before medication, I recovered somewhat. Though my health was not perfect, I did function for a while. I'd like to say that I never experienced episodes like that ever again, but that would not be true.

Nearly fifteen years following the initial diagnosis, I found myself needing inpatient treatment twice in six months because of extreme mania. I was awake for nearly four days straight, paranoid and filled with fear and suicidal ideation, feeling like death would be my only relief. At this time, I even called the suicide hotline. I just didn't feel I had anyone else to turn to who would really understand, or care to listen.

Again, I lost close to twenty pounds in just under two weeks. This was not something I expected to encounter again after years of managing the disease. It happened while I was living in Los Angeles. I'd created an impossible schedule. My life and my condition were simply unmanageable.

I was incredibly stressed, working part-time and going to school full-time. I missed my medication frequently and ultimately went four days with no sleep, barely even blinking. I begged my roommate one night to take me to the emergency room. I was terrified, convinced again that I was being followed while driving and that my phone was tapped. I even went so far as to get one of those burner phones believing it was the only way to talk privately.

In Cleveland my family was supportive and surrounded me with love and support when I was at my worst. They refused inpatient treatment for me in the 90s. Instead, they kept a close eye on me at home, but that was hard as well. I was essentially on lock-down in my own house. The family watched every move I made, ultimately taking my car keys away after I came home with those wild stories. It was better than being alone on the streets like so many who live with this condition, but it was by no means easy, not for any of us.

In LA it was different. Inpatient treatment was the only option, and at that point I was begging to go. I could no longer get around safely to see my doctor on an outpatient basis, and extended family could not advocate for me the way my immediate family did in Cleveland years prior.

I can remember what they told me when I first arrived at that facility. They said I would be in for only three days. When the doctor met with me and heard where my thoughts were going, he suggested I stay the whole week. I agreed, though it was a devastating reality check.

Alone with no one around me but strangers, there was absolutely no human comfort. I had one roommate in a room with empty walls, no decorations, and nothing but twin beds and a bathroom. I think we had one blanket and a pillow. It was hardly glamorous, and when I tell you I cried like I've never cried before, believe it. It was the lowest point in my life.

I kneeled at my bedside and prayed:

"Please God! Heal me and take me from this place. Please let me sleep and wake up healed."

But that is not how it played out. It would be a long road to recovery, and believe it or not, I did not quite yet know what it meant to fully surrender. Stubbornly, I was still white knuckled to my idea of success. I mean, look where I was. Why in God's name would I be thinking about a career? M priorities were so out of line and my faith life was flimsy at best. Where was God? I wondered. I knew He existed but where was He now? How could He leave me in my darkest hour? How could He let me endure this misery? Where did I go wrong and how could I let myself get this bad?

Can you believe I just couldn't see it? I mean it didn't take a rocket scientist to see that I allowed my career ambitions to eclipse my health and even worse, my faith life. It was all such a nasty mess. I felt so alone.

That week I had three visitors: one of my best girlfriends, Sherry, a close cousin, Barbara, and my brother Michael who had been traveling for work. He made an adjustment to his busy schedule to come see his sister, the same sister he stood by the first time she entered outpatient treatment in Cleveland.

The only thing harder than entering this facility was having people see me in this condition. While they all tried to mask their devastation with thinly veiled smiles in an effort to lift my spirits, they weren't successful at convincing me this situation was anything other than grim. I was not very lucid, but I knew by the sick feeling in the pit of my stomach that this indeed was just that, grim.

I didn't want anyone to know I was there, I didn't want my visitors to tell anyone. I knew I could trust them not to gossip. I knew I was safe with them, but I was in a facility I definitely did not feel safe in. How could I? I was surrounded by strangers who were administering new medication that I didn't want to take. I was so frightened.

I do remember however, refusing some of it. Things had changed over the years and patients actually were allowed to say no, believe it or not. I guess I was lucid enough to know I didn't want to be drugged into a catatonic state. These people didn't know me like my personal doctor, and I didn't trust they had my best interest at heart. Thank God, they didn't try to force anything on me that I didn't want to take. At least there was that.

When it was time for each of my visitors to leave, I couldn't bear to see them go. How I wanted to beg them to take me with them, but I had to hold it together. I was too proud to break down in front of them, even though that is exactly what I wanted to do. I held myself together until they left and I went back to my room. That's where I fell apart, hit my knees, again, and begged God to take me from this place.

The medication I did manage to take hadn't helped fully yet. I still could not sleep. I was having a hard time coping with my new surroundings, wanting to leave but also begging for help. Seriously, I would have done just about anything to get some sleep, including enter inpatient treatment for the first time.

The other patients were not what you might expect in a facility like this. No one was violent or resembling characters from *One Flew Over the Cuckoo's Nest*. In fact, there were some very intelligent people there who were afflicted. One woman had a PhD but suffered debilitating depression. This disease does not discriminate. It will attack anyone, young or old, educated or uneducated. She too was in need of the help that neither she nor her higher education could provide. We all needed a place where our medication could be regulated, and where we would have some structure. It was the only thing that would get any of us back on track.

All of our meals, bedtimes and waking hours were scheduled. There was obviously no snacking at our leisure, but we could take naps during the day if we wanted, and if we could actually sleep. I was often told by my doctors in Cleveland that I needed a more structured schedule, but was rarely able to achieve that on my own. This is exactly what inpatient treatment provided.

We were not allowed to have our cell phones. I could not reach out to my family or my friends whenever I wanted. Phone calls had to be scheduled. There was a pay phone in the hallway outside my room. Family and friends had to contact the main number, at which time the person answering would give them the number of that pay phone. We were told when the call could take place, and had to essentially wait in the hallway for it to ring. It was demoralizing.

As much as I would like to provide more details, they just won't come to mind. Though I lived to tell of some of this traumatic experience, I don't think I was meant to see it all for what it was, especially while I was going through it. I think God kept me from processing all of this ugliness at the time. He knew it was just too much. Looking back on it now, it's so evident that God is the only reason I survived this darkness.

As the week ended, I was sent home doing better, though not completely healed. The medication was still not right, but at least I was starting to sleep. They essentially put a bandaid on it all, getting me to sleep but not fixing anything else, including my priorities.

I left there only to resume my hectic schedule, as if oblivious to how it led to me straight to inpatient treatment. Well, being oblivious resulted in being readmitted those six months later, with all the same symptoms magnified. I had just found a new place to live only to leave because I once again, hadn't slept in days. Again, thoughts were racing, my body was dropping a lot of weight in a short amount of time, and the intrusive, paranoid thoughts were back.

This second inpatient treatment gave way to the miracle after which I named this book. Just when I thought that all was lost and never to return, Jesus showed up, literally. My Savior, Provider and Healer did not leave me to fend for myself. On the contrary, He met me in my brokenness, and He is the reason for this testimony you're reading, ultimately leading to my healing.

***

You may have noticed by now that I've said very little about which medications I have been on. There is a very calculated reason for that. Different people react differently to medications. What did or did not work for me, could be the opposite for someone else and I do not want to bias anyone. I will however, go into some detail about my time on lithium, with the hope that it will help someone.

For decades, lithium was the drug of choice for people with bipolar disorder, and with good reason. It worked tremendously well. You could even call it a bit of a life saver. I was on it for years, the doctor at the Cleveland Clinic prescribed it after the efficacy of another drug began to wane. I thrived for a long time on lithium.

The thing about this drug that is so important to realize, is that it can harm your kidneys if you're not careful, which I was for years. The doctor checked my kidney blood work regularly and they were always functioning perfectly. The numbers were always normal. I was not really on enough to cause a problem, until I made a terrible mistake.

I went on a low sodium diet to lose the weight I gained on the meds over the years. While I did lose thirty pounds, I never checked with the doctor beforehand like the diet company recommended. I thought to myself, *"What could be wrong with a low sodium diet?"* Well, there was indeed something very wrong about it.

I neglected to remember that your body needs enough salt if you're taking lithium, because lithium itself is a salt. When it enters your body, it needs to find salt. When it didn't find enough, it spiked to a toxic level and my kidney numbers went way too high. This took a terrible toll on me physically.

I was lithium toxic for nearly two months without knowing it. I went to the doctor three times with flu-like symptoms, indicative of toxicity. They gave me an antibiotic that never worked, because it wasn't the flu. My vision was even beginning to blur. It wasn't until my third trip to the doctor that a nurse practitioner finally put two and two together and discovered what the real problem was. She urged me to go to emergency right away, but I was scared and wanted support. I went home and called my parents. At this point I was weak, sick and with poor vision. I could barely stand anymore. I crawled across the floor to let them in when they arrived. I was living with my boyfriend at the time, but he was working and I couldn't reach him.

They took me to emergency and I was immediately admitted. This began the most painful three days of my life. I was unable to concentrate, feeling so sick, unable to see clearly and feeling incredibly stupid for making this mistake. I should have known better and spoken with my doctor first.

I feared I would end up on dialysis, but thank God, they were able to help me before it got to that point. My doctor was devastated that this happened, though it wasn't really his fault. Had I told him about the diet, he would have warned me about the ramifications. I still look back on this and kick myself.

I was on IV's to flush the drug out of my system, and given another medicine to get my kidneys numbers back down into a normal range. It was so painful when one of the doctors accused me of trying to kill myself by overdosing. My God! Had it really come to this? I begged him to believe that I would never try to actually take my own life. I'm not sure I ever convinced him.

I was released from the hospital to my doctor's care, and had regular blood tests every week for a while, to be sure that my numbers remained stable. Then he took me off the lithium and put me on another medication that I've had great success with, and that I remain on to this day. What an incredibly scary ordeal this was.

Today, while my numbers are stable and much lower, they are not where they ideally should be. I do live with Chronic Kidney Disease as a result of this episode. I don't feel like anything is wrong. While my numbers are not ideal, they are stable, I just have to get them checked regularly, like every couple months. I monitor and control my diet for good renal health, which means being mostly plant based, eating very little animal protein and doing my best to keep my weight down.

It's a lot to take in, I know. I tell my story to help others to not make the same mistake that I did. Lithium is a great drug, and it helped me tremendously. If not for my near fatal error, I would probably still be on it. I was toxic for so long, I am truly lucky to be alive. People literally die from lithium toxicity. You could call it another act of God's undeniable and unbelievable protection. Glory to Him!

***

Over the last forty years, there have been hundreds of medication changes. Sometimes in doses, sometimes in switching drugs all together. No, not everything worked. It was explained very early on in my disease that medication would be a painstaking trial-and-error process until they found the right combination that would allow for a normal life. Treatment is different for everyone.

Initially, the drugs brought me down to earth and healed much of the extreme symptoms, enough to make me more functional and able to work some. The day to day living however, still required a lot of effort and there were emotional scars left with each episode. Invariably, relationships suffered.

Doctors instructed me on self care. They urged regular work outs and eating sensibly, but the more emotional scars I had, the harder it was to get out of my own head long enough to do those things.

The road to health was painful. It was long and had many bumps, twists and turns. I reflected a lot after the trauma I experienced. I couldn't help but recall my childhood and late adolescence. Looking back on the initial diagnosis and what led up to it, I began to see patterns I would eventually learn to break. It unfortunately took much pain and medication to do it however, and it was long before I would learn to be grateful to God.

I see now that He never left, He was just too much of a Gentleman to force Himself into my life. No, He waited, but with His hand on me the whole time. Why couldn't I see it? Was I that far gone?

Indeed I was.

Jesus had something very different and very specific in mind for what would eventually become my testimony. He carefully and lovingly let me fall to the point where the only way out would be through Him and by His immeasurable healing power. That is why *"Tell Them About Me"* is less about me, and more about Jesus.

Reflection Points: Things you can do

Take a moment now and really think about what you've just read. Does it hit home in any way? Where do you find yourself in the midst of your struggle? Do you see someone you love who is struggling?

Has the disease told you that God is not listening? Or maybe you are at a point in your life where you refuse to go to church for that reason. Are you in a lot of pain over it and just don't know what to do? That's where I was. I stopped seeking God because I could not feel His presence anywhere I went. Can you relate?

The truth is that God DID walk with me wherever I went. You might even say He brought the church to me. You read about the things I did, the dangerous places in which I put myself. He HAD to be with me. He put a hedge of protection around me when the disease put me in harms way on multiple occasions. Looking back, this is just one of the many ways I know His presence was real, it's just one of the ways I know the disease lied, and God was indeed always with me.

Are you or is someone you love ignoring medication and burning the wick at both ends? I tried to do everything and failed at all of it. I was driven to my knees. Is this something to which you can also relate? Are you trying relentlessly to make a life for yourself, living in denial that you need help? Yeah, I did that.

Are you experiencing the unbearable highs or devastating lows of bipolar disorder right now? Is someone you love experiencing them? Well, understand that neither of those things can remove the presence of God. Know that whether you are a believer or an unbeliever, Jesus believes that you were worth dying for. Faith is believing what we cannot see, or even feel in our case, especially in our darkest hour.

"When you pass through the waters, I will be with you; and when you pass through the rivers, they will not sweep over you. When you walk through the fire, you will not be burned; the flames will not set you ablaze." —Isaiah 43:2 NIV

"Now faith is being sure of what we hope for and certain of what we do not see. This is what the ancients were commended for." — Hebrews 11:1-3 NIV

I want you to take a moment now, and sit with God. Believe that He is listening to everything you tell Him. What is He saying to you?

Then, go one step further. Take out a journal, and journal to Jesus. I literally call mine my *Jesus Journal* and let me tell you, everything I've ever written to Him has been answered in some capacity. Whether it's your struggle, or the struggle of someone you love and want to help, take the time to sit with God. He has nothing better to do than to hang on your every word! It's impossible for us to get our human brains around, but it is immeasurably true, because He loves us! Just ask the Apostle Paul…

"For I am sure that neither death nor life, nor angels nor rulers, nor things present nor things to come, nor powers, nor height, nor depth, nor anything else in all creation, will be able to separate us from

the love of God in Christ Jesus our Lord." — Romans 8:38-39 ESV

Chapter 2
Growing Up in Brooklyn, Surviving Ohio State

Childhood was not difficult. It was picture-perfect, in fact, to grow up as the youngest of four, doted upon by my siblings and our parents. With two older brothers and an older sister, we were all very close, but my siblings were upwards of ten years older than me. Both brothers played the drums. It was a regular occurrence to hear them blaring their Average White Band records and playing along in the basement. It was pretty cool. My sister and I both sang with my dad, my aunt and cousins in our Byzantine Melkite Greek Catholic Church choir. Still, I was the only one in my immediate family who had a serious side for making music a full-time career.

I was given an abundance of love. Mom and Dad provided a Christian, Catholic foundation that we all remain grateful for today. We have always been a tight knit, ethnic family. My brothers and sister and I were blessed with two very *old school* Lebanese parents.

Mom and Dad put their kids at the center of everything. They lived for two things, their children and their church. They attended nearly every one of my performances all the way through high school and college. While in the Ohio State Scarlet and Gray Show Choir, they managed to drive two hours to Columbus for most shows. Friends used to joke that they would one day actually join the Scarlet and Gray Show. We got such a laugh over that. It was true. They supported everything I did.

Growing up, it would be a typical afternoon to find mom cooking Lebanese food. Whether she had parsley spread out on towels on the kitchen table as she chopped it up to make tabouli, had her hands in meat making kibbeh niyeh, or was picking grape leaves she planted herself, mom was definitely *old school*. Dad did not cook, he never did. He spent much of his time playing music. He kept active playing the drums and singing all over town right up to the end of his life at 92 years of age.

Mom passed away two months prior to their 68th wedding anniversary at age 90, following a long battle with dementia, and Dad a year and a half later following a bad fall from which he never recovered. They each died bedridden. God bless them both, they were faith-filled warriors through what ended up being be very difficult deaths to witness. We all feel strongly that they died in a state of grace, at peace with the Lord, when they drew their last breath. They rest in now glory with our Invisible King. Though we miss them both terribly, this brings with it immeasurable peace.

***

Raised in the Byzantine Catholic Church, no one I grew up with understood the Eastern Rite, which emerged in the Middle East and dates back to well before the east west schism of 1054. My friends were all Catholic, but they came from the Roman Catholic Church.

Within the Byzantine Church is the Melkite Rite. Being American born of Syrian Lebanese and Armenian descent, this is the Rite to which we belonged. It's a beautiful Divine Liturgy, especially the music, filled with harmonic minor, Arabic and Greek music that was passed down orally. There were no basic chord progressions in the Melkite Church, as with the Western. It's lovely, but hard to sing. You really had to tune your ear to the notes in the cracks so to speak. Years later I incorporated some of these beautiful sounds into some jazz music, because I am so proud to be of Arabic descent.

Growing up in a beautifully close, ethnic family laid a happy, loving and faith-filled foundation. It gave me a free spirit that longed to make music, and I did, even as a small child. My family said that I used to sing from my crib upon awakening from naps as a child, but I'll have to take their word for it. The first song I remember singing is *"Close To You,"* by the Carpenters. Karen was my first pop influence.

It was an idyllic life growing up in Brooklyn, Ohio, on the corner of South Parkside and Taunton. We made a home in an orange brick house on a red brick street that Mom and Dad had built. We were the first family to live in it and we stayed from the time I was born until I went off to college. So many of my favorite life memories are stored up in that house: first Christmas, first steps, first birthday, first day of school, first prom and finally, first trip off to college. How many nights I spent sitting on my bed, gazing out the window into this quiet, Midwestern neighborhood, and dreaming of what my life would become. Never did it enter my mind that I might one day be stricken with a disorder that would, quite literally, debilitate me for years.

I had the rare opportunity some thirty years later to visit that house again. It was up for sale, so one day I simply went up to the door and knocked. When the owners answered I told them that this was my first home and I would love the opportunity to walk through it again. I asked when there might be an open house. She told me that it had already been sold but then invited me to come in and look around. I was overjoyed.

As I entered, I couldn't help but comment to myself that the rooms seemed so much smaller than I remembered. Much of the house had changed, like the carpeting, wallpaper, and newly painted rooms, but there were still a number of things that were the same.

Most of the closet doors and door handles had not been replaced and were exactly as I remembered. The red cedar closet in my brother's room still had that woodsy scent. The noisy ceiling fan in the upstairs hallway still rattled, the laundry chute was still there, and so was the rusty old milk chute and mail slot that dropped the mail into the front closet. The linoleum on the stairs leading down to the basement remained, but it was tearing now and I could even see the old floor peeking through.

Upstairs in the bathroom my sister and I shared, there was this pink tile that was all the same. So was the mirror above the sink, and even the soap and toothbrush holders that were cemented into the tiled wall.

Possibly the thing that stood out to me the most growing up, were the marbled stone window sills. Ironically, they were all still there despite the fact that the window treatments had been updated.

I told the owner that I remembered there was one piece of a window sill that used to crack and break off. We would repeatedly pick it up and fit it back in. To my surprise, she told me that the previous owners fixed it, but it broke yet again after they moved in.

"Can I see it?" I asked.

She immediately took me to the room that used to be our dining room. Sure enough, there was that piece of the windowsill that I remember fitting back in every time it fell down.

"Oh my God, it's just like I remembered," I told her. "I can't believe it's still the same after thirty years."

As much as I felt I might be overstepping it, I just had to ask. "Would you mind terribly if I kept this piece of the window sill?"

She hesitated, then said, "Oh sure, I don't see why not."

With that, I now had a piece of the first home I resided in for more than twenty years. It's such a treasure, that I put it in a little wooden treasure chest that I still have in my room with some other very special keepsakes. Before I put it away for safe keeping however, I went over to my piano, placed this special piece of the marble stone windowsill on it, and began to write a song. It was about my first house and the memories it stored. Actually, the song *"This Old House"* kind of wrote itself.

Many of the surrounding families in this neighborhood still live there. Two best friends of mine lived right across the street. When I wasn't in my room practicing the flute or singing along with my favorite Barbra Streisand records, I was sure to be found with them. We were either climbing trees or playing Ghost in the Graveyard, which was a lot like hide and seek.

If you were "it" in Ghost In The Graveyard, you had to stay stationary, like on someone's porch. Everyone else could run around anywhere they wanted, trying to stay out of sight. It was your job to spot them and call out their name and location.

"I see Nancy behind the tree on Richard's tree lawn," or something like that.

Once you were caught, you had to sit on the porch with your captor. The catch in Ghost In The Graveyard was that you could be saved. If someone could make it to the porch without being called out, they could free the captives. So if you were it, you tried to spot everyone before they could be set free. Oh yeah, the best part of Ghost In The Graveyard is that it was only played at night. It was just one of the cool things that we did to pass the hours.

We also went on epic long bike rides. We were gone for hours. When we returned and it was time for dinner, our parents would yell from the front porches until we came running. We could always count on dinner as a family growing up. As kids, we also swam at the community pool until our skin was wrinkled and our eyes were bloodshot. I was a diver and a synchronized swimmer. We caught lightning bugs at night in the summer, then we laid on the ground and stared up at the sky counting stars. Actually, we did this in the daytime too, only then we were looking at clouds, trying to find the angel hair, and ice cream castles of which Joni Mitchell would sing.

It was a simpler time. The music on the radio was so different from what it is today. I just loved listening to Joni, who was all over the radio growing up in the seventies, as was Carole King, James Taylor, Stevie Wonder, Aretha Franklin, Ambrosia, Teena Marie, Stevie Nicks, and many others. They are still some of my musical heroes, and she-roes, and they all sparked the early desire in me to one day become a singer/songwriter.

Dad also raised me on Ella Fitzgerald and Frank Sinatra, the Dorsey brothers and the Glenn Miller Orchestra, Joe Williams, Matt Monroe, Doris Day, Rosemary Clooney and so many other crooners of the day. I was just raised on good music.

When Dad realized he was raising a budding singer, he started taking me to his gigs. He had me sit in with his band, but only after teaching me to know what key I would sing a song in and how to count it off at the proper tempo. He was my first teacher. As a child of nine or ten years old, I was ahead of some professionals as a result.

Singing wasn't my only craft. As I said, I was a flutist and began to play in the fourth grade. Taking to it instantly, I always played first chair in school ensembles and received superior ratings in the yearly solo and ensemble competitions. I went on to receive a music scholarship from Ohio State University but later dropped it for a Journalism degree. My degree program had been music education, until I could no longer visualize myself chained to a classroom for a living. The desire for that kind of career didn't come until thirty years later.

As an adolescent, my first job was to babysit for the neighbors' children, and the parents of all of my friends knew me well. It was a real neighborhood. I ran, jumped and swam like the healthy girl that I was. I went to church every Sunday with my whole family. Life was not complicated back then.

The only thing that gave way to some abnormality as a teenager, was the frequent need for an inordinate amount of sleep, getting at least ten hours per night in the summer, then nap during the day. Ironically once the school year began, I did not sleep much at all, running myself ragged and burning the candle at both ends. My life lacked balance from a very early age, and it always concerned my parents, who were never able to convince me to slow down.

There were band practices, show choir rehearsals, play practices and preparations for those solo and ensemble contests, barely making time for homework which caused much stress. Mom and dad tried, I just didn't know how to slow down. All I understood was how to push myself until I practically dropped. Unfortunately, this behavior continued for the rest of my life, and it really hurt me terribly once I began to battle bipolar disorder. Perhaps it was even a very early sign of the disease, even before that first major episode.

Still, I earned good grades, and advanced in Language Arts. I took Advanced Placement English in High School, and I was in so many plays and musicals that I became a Thespian.

The need for that much sleep was later attributed to two autoimmune disorders: Alopecia Areata (hair loss in patches), and an enlarged thyroid (Hashimoto's). For the record, autoimmune disorders can really wreak havoc on a person. Alopecia makes one's immune system attack the hair follicle, causing it to fall out. The endocrinologist at the Cleveland Clinic told us it was a genetic disease usually triggered by stress, of which I had much. Early on, it fell out in small patches.

The first time this happened was in the second grade, when I had just learned that my teacher, Mrs. Elzholse, had died. She was literally here today, gone tomorrow. It confused all her students, especially me. This was an emotional trigger that put stress on my body. That was the first time a little bald patch appeared, but it went away with some cortisone cream. Years later however, this conditioned worsened tremendously, and the treatments went from applying cortisone cream, to getting painful cortisone injections in my head that would eventually stop working.

At 26 years old, my sister Denise was helping me get dressed for a New Year's Eve party that I would be singing. As she did my hair, she noticed several bald patches in close proximity at the crown of my head. Little by little, those small patches turned into one large bald spot, soon requiring a fall, or partial wig to cover it up.

Mom and I went back to this endocrinologist who promptly assured me that I would not lose all of my hair. Through a beautiful thick Eastern Indian accent, he was actually very reassuring.

"Don't worry, Miss Jacobs, you are not going to lose all of your hair. This is not going to happen. It will all grow back."

Sadly, he was wrong. We returned several weeks later with only a few strands of hair left. What did he have to say? If not so sad it would be funny.

"Yes Miss Jacobs, you are losing all of your hair."

"Oh, really?" I replied with a note of sarcasm in my voice. I wanted to say, "Do you really think so, Captain Obvious?" But the tears kept me from saying another word.

Alopecia in any form is hereditary. An uncle on my dad's side had it, but he was much older and in poor health when the onset occurred. He lost all of his hair inside of a week. His trigger was physical stress, as he was taking some new medication. He used to wake up in the morning and there would be hair all over his bed.

Similarly, I used to sit in my one-bedroom apartment in a big, comfy chair with a large white pillow across my lap. As I ran my fingers through the thick, black, coarse strands, it easily came out in large clumps that I placed on the pillow. I don't have to tell you what kind of stress this caused.

There are four types of Alopecia: Androgenetic or a thinning of hair; Areata which is loss of patches of hair; Totalis, the loss of all the hair on your head, and Universalis, the total loss of all the hair on your head and body. This final form is where I was now. Eyebrows were thinning, eyelashes were falling out, leg hair, nose hair, everything. It was dramatic and caused depression.

The first time I tried on a full wig however, everything changed. Much of the stress and depression lifted. The wigs were beautiful, and the best part was, they didn't look like wigs. I was much more comfortable within my own skin and no longer had to stress about trying desperately to cover up bald patches.

I was blessed with a family to go through it with me, and the people who made the wigs had great bedside manners. Mom and dad were quick to remind me how much worse it could be. After all, I tried on wigs in the same room with cancer patients who not only lost their hair, but who were also fighting for their lives.

"Someone always has it worse honey," my mother and father would say. "Just be thankful and trust the Lord. He will take care of everything."

God bless my parents. They were teaching me about faith every day.

Music became even more of a release. Little by little I was becoming a bit of a teenage recluse, spending hours in my room practicing and cultivating the craft of music, which later in life, became the life-saving gift from God which would eventually bring me closer to Him.

Unlike a lot of teenagers in high school and later in college, partying and drinking did not thrill me. I got my kicks playing music. Early on it was the flute, then in college I became more serious about singing professionally. That hooked me on music even more, while simultaneously dealing with the onset of bipolar disorder. The love of the gift severely eclipsed love for the Giver, leaning heavily on music, not God. Oh sure, I believed in God and I loved Jesus, but I had not yet learned to put Him at the center of all that I did.

Filled with self-will, all I wanted was to perform for large audiences, make records and at the time, get signed by a record label. That's how it was back then. There were no independent artist platforms like there are today. I was convinced that if I just had a big career, everything else would fall into place. I was convinced that a career would cure and heal me. I never stopped to consider that what I really needed was a closer walk with Jesus. It took years to realize that the path He would put before me, in His own time, would be better than anything I could dream up for myself. I just couldn't see it yet. It took years of pain before my faith would evolve to the point of complete surrender to God; pain that would begin in my late adolescence, and stay with me for decades.

***

Emotionally abusive relationships are a real thing for some people. What draws us into relationships that are harmful and devaluing? It probably has a lot to do with the fact that they don't start out that way.

While in college the first time at Ohio State, I met someone who pursued me to a degree that I could not ignore, and to the point where everyone around us knew that he was interested. I became taken with him and it scared me, because I already had a boyfriend. I was young and had never known a situation like this. It was dramatic. I felt things for him that I hadn't felt for my boyfriend in a long time. He had just graduated, and we were now apart quite a bit. In walked this new love interest, and he was a head turner. Little did I know that the intoxicating infatuation we shared for each other would soon turn into conflict and discord, the earliest of which stemmed from my need for privacy.

It really angered him that I insisted we didn't go public with our feelings for each other early on, for fear my boyfriend would find out, as I didn't want to hurt him. He wanted to shout it to the world, but I kept putting the brakes on, and I think he took that personally.

Still, I felt that I couldn't possibly have such strong feelings for someone else if I was truly meant to be with my existing boyfriend, and I eventually broke up with him after two years of dating. It was a rapid decision and very out of character. I literally pulled the old cut and run. I was blinded by what I eventually came to learn was nothing more than intense infatuation, which I mistook for love.

Once I did break up with my boyfriend, we did go public with our relationship, which was very short lived. It was a whirlwind romance. I think we dated for a total of four months, the first half of which were, as I said, intoxicating.

In the beginning, he brought me flowers, took me to concerts, and told me I was beautiful. I was over the moon.

It was not long however, before the emotional abuse would begin. Communication was just not his thing. He resorted to hurtful, sarcastic comments when difficult situations arose. They penetrated an already fragile and emotional soul, who took everything he said to heart, a broken heart at that. The more we got to know each other, the more diminutive he became of everything that mattered to me.

He ridiculed my Catholic faith, and my closeness with my family. He contributed to an already distorted body image by making negative comments about my shape. He was especially diminutive about my music. Like many in emotionally abusive relationships, I blamed myself and tried to be someone he would want to stay with. Instead, I watched him slowly disappear.

To make matters even more dramatic, he was not a Christian and back then, I was still very devoted to my faith. I was confused about falling for someone who was of a different faith practice, but trying to talk to him about it was fruitless. He literally shamed me for thinking this could be a problem down the road if we didn't address it now. In fact, we couldn't really talk about anything important.

What we felt was a lot of physical attraction that I was hesitant to act on before our relationship could fully evolve into something real. We never had what my first boyfriend and I had. We just never got that far. On the contrary, the more our differences were exposed, the more I faced a barrage of mean, toxic and sarcastic comments from him.

We were so different. I wanted to talk things through, but he didn't, or he couldn't. In his defense, I think this was difficult for him too, but he was also young, and had no idea how to handle the tensions we were facing.

Before we officially broke up, he was starting to date a mutual friend. It was summer and we were all performers at a theme park. We were together all the time. I could not separate myself from this painful situation. Though they were trying to hide their budding relationship, our fellow performers found out and could not keep a secret. When the news got back to me, sadness and profound despair cast a dark shadow over my soul, and my mental health.

To make matters worse, our so-called friends in their infinite compassion, made jokes and had fun with all of us. They even put on a Saturday Night Live style skit at a party, portraying each of us as characters, acting out our love triangle. Ouch, that was excruciating. I suppressed my devastation in public, only to fall apart and sob uncontrollably when alone. It was my first real heartbreak. I did not have the emotional constitution to handle it. Depression began to overtake me, and I just could not recover.

Sadness was to be expected, but the doctors said that the lasting depression was the rearing of bipolar disorder's ugly head. It is important to know that this trying situation was a trigger, not a cause, as bipolar disorder was genetic in my case.

By now my life had changed dramatically. No longer myself, I enjoyed nothing but singing, which became music therapy. There were still emotional ramifications from this breakup which never seemed to end. They took on a life of their own.

On campus, rather than lighting up when I walked in the room like he used to, he was dark, negative and he tried to avoid me. It was an excruciating sting when I would walk over to him, only to have him look me dead in the eye, turn his back, and walk out of the room. It was an emotional 180 on his part, and it left an unshakable residue on me, not to mention how embarrassing it was. Everyone knew how he had pursued me only four short months ago. Now they were all asking 'what happened to those two?' and gossiping. Yes, so much for privacy, which was even more important to me after our breakup.

I strongly believed that he was disparaging when he talked about our brief tenure as a couple. I was interpreting people so differently now. Thoughts were dark and rarely rooted in reality. They were broken. This is how the disease manifested. I took his emotionally abusive behavior to heart, and couldn't let it go, not even after our break up. So self-focused, I convinced myself that everyone was criticizing me and taking behind my back. My nerves were raw.

It's possible there was some truth in that notion; people do like to talk after all. Looking back while healthy however, I hardly think it was as bad as it appeared at the time. Unfortunately, prior to living in remission, this kind of paranoid thought pattern was prominent throughout my life as I navigated the rough terrain of living with bipolar disorder. I developed the defense mechanism of projecting my feelings onto others.

This was about the time that it became difficult to go to church. There was an extreme sensitivity to the interfaith component within our brief relationship, for both of us. He was indeed shaming when the subject came up. That was most definitely real. It all took its toll on my faith, causing depression and tears throughout the Catholic Mass, so I stopped going. These depressive episodes seemed to last forever, and they were compounded by the fact that no matter how I begged God to heal me, I was still sick, for years.

There were signs of suicidal thoughts when I would run into friends on campus and talk of long hallways and dead-end signs. I think some people knew that there was something really wrong. They questioned my comments and behavior, but bipolar disorder is cyclical. I was not always in a mood state or fully episodic, but still by no means fine. The disease is a bit of a moving target and for this reason, it was difficult for anyone to know exactly what I was going through or when it occurred

While sharing an apartment with two male friends, they had no idea what was wrong with me, but then again, neither did I. It was finals week and they kept trying to get me to study but I couldn't. Obviously, I was impaired and gave up.

Singing proved to be a welcome distraction from mounting emotional pain and mental anguish, even if only temporarily. So, I did more of it. The singers in town were generous to share the bandstand. The only downside to this oasis of mine was the fact that I still feared everyone in town was gossiping about my erratic behavior. Bipolar disorder is a very self-centered disease.

I later learned that this kind of thinking, these paranoid thoughts, are called persecutory delusions. They are textbook symptoms of bipolar disorder.

It didn't help that I managed to do something really embarrassing. I went to a friend's recital one night. It was not in a recital hall, but rather a cafeteria area, seeming a bit informal. From where I was sitting, I could not see the professors who were grading him. My friend, who was in the middle of playing a guitar solo, simply looked at me and smiled. Mistakenly believing it was an invitation, I got up from my seat looking disheveled, went to the bandstand, and began to sing the song.

The looks on the professors faces were horrifying. They were wondering what I was doing. I was so out of it. It was an example of this self-centered disease, thinking everything was about me. I was completely out of place and it gave people something to talk about.

I suppose if I had to do something really wrong, singing when not invited wasn't the worst thing, even if it was someone's recital. I went home afterwards, still not believing that I did anything out of character. That same musician friend came over later that night to see what was wrong. I was talking in circles, but he was kind. He could see something was terribly wrong, but he didn't judge.

Unfortunately, the word spread and now people were definitely talking about my behavior at that recital. I had, after all, given them much to discuss. Finally, a friend called my parents to tell them I was doing some strange things and that something was really wrong. In turn, they called me to see what was going on.

They were distracted from the erratic behavior that friend had told them about once they realized that I flunked out that quarter. I didn't know how to tell them that I had been depressed and just could not concentrate on my studies. How could I, when I didn't even understand myself?

At that time, they just didn't realize that there was a much bigger issue at work. They knew I was going out and singing. They put together the only pieces they could see, and they didn't like it.

Tell Them About Me

"You failed your classes because you didn't go to class and you didn't study. You went out to sing," my mother exclaimed.

"I just couldn't," I told her.

She wasn't buying it, neither was my father, though he tried to be calm and diplomatic.

Eventually, they did see that something was very wrong. My sister helped in this area, advocating for me as she always did. After a heart to heart talk, she understood much better than our parents did. Isn't that what big sisters are for?

"Why didn't you tell us sooner you were having trouble? Why did you wait until you were failing all of your classes?" She asked.

"I thought I did," I told her.

"Well, you didn't, not until it was too late to do anything."

So, the two of us decided to tell mom and dad that it was best to come home for a quarter. As hard as it was to go home to live with my parents again after being on my own at school, there was just nothing else left to do. I left Ohio State spring quarter, 1990. That's when the real fun began.

***

I returned home the antithesis of the girl my parents sent away. They now saw me emaciated, thin and gaunt. I was depressed and fully manic at the same time, something doctors later called mixed states. It was the first time my weight dropped significantly in just a week or two.

One minute I was sad and crying, the next minute giddy and glib, up and down like a roller coaster. Now they were seeing first hand the strange things I was saying and doing and they were scared. I was moody and irritable. The severity of those paranoid thoughts began to worsen. I kept telling my parents that our phone was tapped and I was unable to concentrate on anything, talking in circles.

My parents, being devout Catholics, prayed for healing. They strongly believed in the power of prayer and the church, so that's the first place they took me. Mom lit candles while dad asked the priest for his blessing for his ailing daughter. Unfortunately, this was not something that could be prayed away. I came to learn later that many churches kind of sweep mental illness under the rug. Some even believe that depression and manic depression are sent by the devil and do not require medical attention, but rather, spiritual healing. I encountered this a bit years later in LA.

Then came all the questions.

"Maria, have you gotten into drugs? Did you get pregnant? Did you have an abortion?"

"No, No, NO!" I screamed at my mother. "Why are you asking me this?"

"You're just not yourself and we don't know what to do with you," she replied.

"What do you mean our phone is tapped? What has been going on at Ohio State?" Mom asked more than once, hoping for the lucid answer she would never receive.

They became worried, even devastated by something that clearly had no easy fix. They felt helpless, as any parent would.

It was later that a musician friend recommended a psychologist. He was good, and I saw him a couple of times a week. Mom and dad were not interested in the idea of therapy. They could see that something was not right, but they were still in denial that treatment was necessary. It took my sister and brother to convinced them.

"Alright," my mother said. "You can go to therapy, but no psychiatrists. I don't want you on any of that medication."

So that summer, off to therapy I went. It was not easy to tell a complete stranger the intimate details of my life. He was hearing my broken thoughts. I told him that nothing seemed real, everything seemed fake. I was connecting dots between people and situations that had nothing to do with each other and that fueled more persecutory delusions. Or was it the other way around? Either way, I felt cut off from the world.

These were all indications to him that I was bipolar. He knew from the start that I needed a psychiatrist, but my parents absolutely refused, and I wasn't well enough to find one on my own. My brother went to that first appointment with me. It was impossible to process what the psychologist was instructing in my current state, but Michael got the picture.

After a few weeks in talk therapy, though not yet medicated, my folks pushed me to get more active. They insisted I either get a job or take summer classes. The doctor agreed that I should do whatever I could to avoid sitting around and thinking, letting my thoughts get the better of me. I went to a community college to take a nine-credit hour, intensive history class. I was trying to catch up after flunking out at Ohio State. What a miserable summer that was.

I finally went back to school in the fall. This was much to the dismay of the psychologist, who still recommended I see a psychiatrist who could prescribe medication.

I got through that first full cycle of depression and mania by the skin of my teeth. I returned to school and hooked up with a student therapist who needed a certain amount of time working with patients in order to graduate. Those sessions were painfully worthless. He had no real experience. You could say that I was a bit of a guinea pig.

A year later, when the disease fully cycled again, I returned home displaying all the same symptoms as before only far worse, if you can believe that.

I went back to my psychologist who insisted on a psychiatrist so that she could prescribe the medication I so needed. At this point, my family agreed, even my parents.

At that first appointment with her, I was in the middle of a depressive cycle. After only about ten minutes in her office, she took out her prescription pad, believing that was the only issue.

She prescribed 150 milligrams of an antidepressant, giving no credence to the manic symptoms I was also experiencing because they weren't present at that particular moment. She missed a lot, rushing to the wrong medication before gathering all the information.

This doctor was one of those who had some mental health issues of her own, like many who find their way into a field like psychology or psychiatry. Because of their own issues, they feel they can be of help to others. Often times, doctors like this are the most empathetic. This is absolutely true in many cases, just not with her. She really had no business in this line of work. She misdiagnosed me and as a result, I endured more mania.

We deeply regretted not getting a second opinion. Going on medication is not a process to enter into lightly. After all, if someone was diagnosed with a serious form of cancer and was told they needed surgery right away, they would get a second opinion, right?

Where medications are concerned, people should ask a lot of questions of more than one doctor. The problem is, if someone is afflicted and alone, they are not able to do that kind of probing. They fall through the cracks. This is why it is so important to have someone who can advocate for you through this difficult process. I had a strong support network and we still got burned.

Doctors are not perfect, they're human and they make mistakes. That's why they call it *practicing* medicine. This woman however, was an absolute criminal. Years later she was arrested and sent to prison for misusing and abusing opioid prescriptions. She really hurt a lot of people, not just me.

Because of her misdiagnosis, I found myself in a real downward spiral. Those paranoid thoughts worsened, cycling back and forth rapidly. I was driving erratically, speeding ninety miles down the freeway at one point. I didn't trust anyone and the relationship with my family was strained to say the least. I didn't believe they were trying to help me. I was mistakenly convinced they wanted to hurt me, at one point believing they were taking money from my checking account to keep me dependent on them. The disease told a lot of lies like that. I feared them. I feared everyone.

Let's face it, none of us had any idea what manic depressive illness was. So there we all were, trying to navigate through a situation that none of us understood. We were crying, yelling, and arguing. I didn't want to be there but I could not be on my own. I was stuck, trying unsuccessfully to get well and I was difficult to be around.

They were watching closely again and it was impossible to bear. I snuck out alone to do what I loved to do, sing. They didn't want me going into bars in the state I was in for fear I would drink to self-medicate. This was a common malady among people with bipolar disorder, but it was not an issue for me until many years later.

Singing, however, was relief at the time and bars were where the music was. That's where I went despite their warnings and concerns. I didn't have any other self-help tools. The disease told me God was not listening, so I stopped seeking Him.

Then my brother found a God send. Michael was in medical sales. He had clients in the world-renowned Cleveland Clinic. He asked one of the doctors who would be able to help his sister with what we were all told was manic depressive illness. That doctor quickly recommended a wonderful psychiatrist.

He was the head of the Mood Research Department, and he really knew what he was doing. My condition was becoming more and more difficult to treat because I was not simply experiencing mood swings. There was paranoia and impaired reality testing, and it was all difficult to treat, as it would clearly take more than one medication to help everything. It was he who recognized right away that an antidepressant alone would do more harm than good. I was in need of more, and that road was rocky at best.

It was painstaking finding the right medication, but as imperfect as the process was early on, it got so much better. Without treatment and medication, life would just not have been worth living. It would have been nice if one prescription would have solved everything indefinitely, but the medication changes with the cycles of the disease. It's just not an if/then equation. You don't just take one tablet of lithium and boom, all is well. This is not how it works, at least not for Bipolar 1 Disorder.

Whether increasing or decreasing doses, or replacing one drug with another, I have gone through hundreds of medication changes over the last 40 years, but the important thing to remember is that I found a brilliant, conscientious, and attentive psychiatrist and psychologist at the Cleveland Clinic. They were a team. I went to one for psychopharmacology, and the other for talk therapy. That is how the system worked.

It's been a painful life, but also one filled with blessings. Some who struggle with bipolar disorder have no family, no support network, and they never find good doctors; they never learn to seek God They end up homeless or worse. I had all of the above. God never left me alone, though for a long time it felt like He had.

I probably should have had inpatient treatment in Cleveland all those years ago, but my family couldn't bear to think of it. They really did have my back despite how difficult this was for all of us.

Truth be told, it all could have been much worse. I was given every opportunity to win this excruciatingly difficult battle which today, I have finally done, thanks be to God. Because of Him, I can tell my story and give Him all the glory. He healed through medication and the right doctors, giving me a unique testimony. This is why *Tell Them About Me*, is less about me, and more about Jesus!

Reflection Points: Things you can do

Take a few minutes now and think about what you've just read. Does anything in this chapter strike a chord with you? God blessed me, even at this backwards time in my life. That's the definition of Grace. He was immeasurably patient, as it took a long time to be obedient and seek His true Will. That's the definition of Mercy. God carved out His perfect plan for my life and led me in His Divine Providence that today has me feeling eternally grateful.

Where do you find yourself right now in the healing process? Are you between doctors? Do you find that you are not receiving the kind of help that you need? Is the medication you're taking just not working like you'd hoped it would? I understand, I was there. I suffered setbacks as well, but I found the right doctors, and so can you. Ask God to reveal the proper care that will set you on the right path.

Loved ones, as you advocate for someone in your life who is struggling, don't stop looking for the right doctor (s). Bring God into the process and ask Him to reveal the one(s) that will be right for them. Attentive, caring and empathetic doctors exist. They are out there, but it's a process.

I cannot explain why God heals some with the wave of His hand, and others through doctors and treatment. All I can say is, if He puts you on the treatment path, it's because He wants to use you too to testify to His glory, grace and mercy through it all. Anyone can praise God when it's good, but praising Him when we are in the midst of a struggle, now that's a testimony. The truth is, we are all being called to take up our cross and follow Him.

I am in remission today with medication. God healed me mentally and physically, but most importantly, He healed me spiritually. Never discount the spiritual healing just because you may still have an ailment. Just trust that everything you are living right now, be it easy or difficult, God will use for your good and His glory.

"And we know that in all things God works for the good of those who love Him, who have been called according to His purpose."
— Romans 8:28 NIV

Finally, don't forget to journal. As I said in chapter one, everything I've ever journaled to Jesus, has come to fruition. As you sit quietly with Him, take some time and write the things you want to say or ask Him. Journaling to Jesus can be effective, especially when we read it back to ourselves aloud. Think of it as writing out your own, well thought out, personalized prayers from you to Him. Jesus will appreciate it, and He will answer. No postage required, just the sincerity of your heart.

Chapter 3
On the Radio

It took three years to save enough money to move to LA. In the early to mid-90s, I worked as a traffic reporter for some of the biggest radio and television stations in Cleveland. Family and friends were tickled hearing my voice on the radio every morning. My brothers and my sister were so proud when their friends would call them and ask,

"Was that Maria I heard on the radio this morning? She sounds great, what an exciting career she has!"

Everyone assumed it was a glamorous job. They assumed I had a glamorous life. The truth was however, it was rough holding down several jobs at that time, one as a full-time traffic reporter, another as a part-time disc jockey for another station on weekends, and the other as a waitress. Between the three, I managed to make a living with a somewhat public life in the early stages of my diagnosis.

At one point early on in my traffic tenure, amidst much professional stress, I found myself working through a pretty rough manic episode. I did not require inpatient treatment; I was doing outpatient treatment at the Cleveland Clinic at the time.

I wasn't sleeping much with this difficult schedule, and I began dealing again with many of those intrusive, disruptive and disordered thoughts, which did tend to resurface with stress. I was depressed and reliving a traumatic past, certain that people were working against me in my current profession. Medication was being adjusted and that made me oversleep nearly every morning. In addition, it caused a fairly significant amount of weight gain, and that alone caused self-loathing and more depression. Truth be told, I struggled with a poor body image most of my life, but most especially after I began taking medication.

My work schedule was not conducive to a balanced lifestyle. I needed to be at work by 5:30 am and it was not uncommon to find me dashing in the door at 5:29. It irritated my colleagues, rightfully so, but they had no idea what was going on behind the scenes. It was anything but glamorous.

The traffic job paid a meager thirteen thousand dollars a year. The office we broadcast from was a run down little room with coffee stained, smelly carpeting. Eight of us were crammed into the same room behind our individual, pathetic little cubicles. Smelly carpet and substandard pay not withstanding, the job did have its merits.

I was the traffic voice for the legendary, flagship station WMMS. It was a bit of a dream, having practically grown up listening to them. I made so little money however; I had to live with my parents. I needed them, and they were there for me, as they always were. Still, I was twenty-three years old and anxious for a stable, independent life of my own. I was relentlessly striving to get ahead professionally as a singer and broadcaster, frequently allowing my career ambitions to eclipse my health. I didn't have the career I ultimately wanted. I was not a singer with a large, national audience and I was down on myself much of the time as a result. I wasn't exactly counting my blessings.

There were a few ego builders and perks along this difficult road. I frequently sang the National Anthem for the Indians, Cavs, and Browns. The hosts had a kick with this on their morning show, airing those recordings and promoting my gigs. Friends from high school whom I hadn't seen in years, even those who ignored me back in the day, saw me around town and treated me like I was the bell of the ball. Yeah, I guess it was fun being a bit of a local celebrity.

***

One of the most memorable experiences as an on-air traffic reporter, was walking through the Rock and Roll Hall of Fame on the day it opened. I was given a press pass to this huge, and memorable event, and I do mean huge.

There were thousands of people lining the streets, watching the Rock and Roll parade march down East Ninth Street. We listened to Yoko Ono and Little Richard speak to the enthusiastic, Rock hungry crowd. Their voices bellowed gleefully through the giant, tower-like speakers in celebratory fashion. Afterwards, we all caught an ear glimpse of Rock legends doing a marathon concert at the jam packed Cleveland Municipal Stadium. It was a happening all the way around.

When the doors opened, I was awe-struck walking through this beautiful building. It was hallowed ground. At one point, I found myself walking along side of the Godfather of Soul and his bodyguards. They were keeping people back, but somehow I was lucky enough to meet the iconic James Brown and shake his hand. I guess you could say we exchanged pleasantries. I extended my hand and said,

"Hi James."

He nodded, looked me in the eye and said,

"Uh huh."

Well, it was pleasant for me anyway. Though brief, meeting the self-proclaimed *'hardest working man in show business,'* was still a thrill. Shortly after, I met the legendary producer and co-founder of Atlantic Records, Ahmet Ertegun. He spoke to a small room filled with reporters and other radio personalities. I considered slipping him my demo tape but thought, nah, not exactly the best time. I had guts back then, but I wasn't stupid.

It was just all so surreal. Literally everyone who was anyone was there that day. It was an historic occasion and I was thrilled to have just a small part in it. It was such a fun time to be working in Cleveland radio, but it was also a grueling schedule that in the long run, didn't do much for my condition.

The traffic reports aired during early morning and afternoon drive times. I waitressed lunch in between shifts at a popular and nearby downtown restaurant, the East 9th Street Grill. We broadcast the traffic from Reserve Square which was walking distance away.

My daily schedule meant up at 4:30 in the morning, on the air from 5:30 to 9:30, and waitressing from 11:00 until 2:30. Then the afternoon drive began at 3:00 and went until 6:00. As if that weren't enough, I disc jockeyed from 2 am to 6 am Sunday mornings on Cleveland's Wave station, and took singing gigs whenever possible.

Yes, it was grueling, but also liberating at the start. Since the onset of my condition, this marked the first time my health would allow me to hold down a full-time schedule, which eventually took its toll. I was so hungry for success, I would take any job I could to get ahead as a broadcaster and singer.

Everyday I walked to the restaurant where I waitressed, I passed the beautiful and historic St. John's Cathedral. I frequently went in to just sit alone and pray. I loved being in that church alone. It was so peaceful and quiet. There was no emotional noise that I frequently felt when surrounded by people. I could just meditate on Christ, talk to Him, and pray with no interruptions, just me and Jesus, as I tried hard to rebuild the Faith life that had been crippled by bipolar disorder and past traumas.

I would gaze at the beautiful stained glass windows which depicted biblical scenes like the Annunciation, the Nativity, the Resurrection and the Ascension of our Lord. It was the only time I could be still, all the while seeking that *"peace beyond all understanding,"* spoken of in Philippians 4:7. It was so hard to find in my chaotic life at the time. If I had only realized how important it was to have more quiet time with Jesus. Life was so noisy, and I rarely sought the quiet for long. When I did, it was at St. John's Cathedral for just a few minutes in between jobs.

It was a welcome break from a difficult life. I was usually praying that the disease would not resurface. I was raised to believe that God hears every prayer, but the condition still caused me to cycle, especially when dealing with the stress I frequently put on myself. This happened during my traffic tenure.

My health was spotty and my medications were changing. Since one of the side effects was fatigue, my sister took me to work on occasion, so that I didn't have to drive. She was astonished at how I was able to effectively do the job live on the air with all that I was enduring behind the scenes. Mine was a common scenario of a creative who was one hundred percent on their game while doing the job, but falling apart as soon as the microphone was off.

I can remember going into my boss's office at one point in tears, telling him I could not work anymore, but I couldn't articulate why. How can one articulate those disruptive, disordered, intrusive, and nagging, depressive thoughts? It was a cycle similar to the one I lived through in college just a few years prior. I was again, filled with fear. I don't know how else to describe it.

I begged him to let me go home in mid shift. He was baffled, but he obliged me and took over my shift himself. That was not yet the end of my traffic reporting career. As my health improved, I was able to return and thankful he would have me back.

Once I got past this difficult depressive and manic cycle, I hit the ground running. I began to push myself again. I took on another disc jockey job at the public radio station, WCPN, and later became a research assistant there on some weeknights. Would you believe throughout all of this radio work I also found time to sing? I did.

I was just so driven. With every set back came the determination to make up for lost time. I wanted a better life, so I pushed myself harder and harder. My weekends were exhausting, then my hectic schedule resumed during the week. I ignored everyone's advice to take it slow, including that of my doctors. They wanted me on a more structured schedule, allowing for regular sleep and time to plan healthy meals and workouts, which I was not doing. I struggled with my weight from the time I began medication. I still struggle with it today. Weight gain has been a consistent struggle of mine for years, but truth be told, I've had food struggles all my life. The medication just made them worse.

My health may have required a more structured environment, but my artistic spirit did not. So I pressed on with the hectic schedule that included overnight shifts, waitressing, full-time traffic reporting on a split shift and singing whenever I could. That went on for about two years before my professional life changed dramatically.

My traffic reporting career ended abruptly when they forbade me to pursue a golden career opportunity. 106.5 FM, the soft rock station that we did traffic for, was looking for a female co-host for their new morning show. Everyone was vying for that position, including another traffic reporter with whom I worked.

I knocked on the proverbial locked door for weeks, until I finally got up the gumption to go to the station in person. I told the receptionist that I was there to meet with the program director. I knew he would remember my name because I was calling nearly every day to get a meeting with him. I got lucky, for a minute.

He agreed to see me, and after a few minutes of glaring at me, asking what the hell I was thinking showing up unannounced, he gave me a shot. He decided that I had guts and moxy, and guts and moxy were exactly what he was looking for in a female co-host.

He suddenly went from ignoring my phone calls to offering me a live, on-air audition, making me one of five finalists for the job. They were auditioning a new person each day for a week. I was to sit in with the new morning show team for an entire morning drive, to see if I would fit in. I was thrilled and astonished at the same time. I went from having no chance, to being in the top five, thinking to myself, "*I love this business.*"

I immediately went to my boss and told him I needed Wednesday morning off, and I told him why. He agreed, at first. He even congratulated me. So here I was, poised to advance my radio career. It was everything I was working toward in my broadcast career. Then came a rough break.

My boss called his boss, who heartlessly put the kibosh on the whole thing, stating it was against my no compete clause to audition, much less get the job. What a letdown. This infuriated me. After all, I wasn't in radio to be a traffic reporter my whole life. It was a stepping stone for exactly this kind of opportunity.

I essentially told my boss I didn't care about my no compete clause, and I was going to audition anyway. Confident I had a tremendous shot at being hired, I was willing to give up my traffic job, even before I knew for sure that I would get the position. That's how much I wanted a shot, and I was at peace with it all. Sadly, the program director at 106.5 was not. He didn't want to burn a bridge with the traffic center, so he refused to follow through with his invitation to audition.

I was disgruntled to say the least, and in protest, I quit the traffic center. This finally ended my traffic reporting career in Cleveland. I was heartbroken. Rather than wallow, I picked myself up by the bootstraps, and continued to disc-jockey part-time on weekends, while seeking a more substantially paying job. I found my way to selling cellular phones and pagers. It was far from artistic, and I felt like a sell-out, but I made enough money to make my first CD and eventually, move to LA.

I worked full-time at this sales job during the week, and disc jockeyed on weekends, hanging on to my radio dream by my finger nails, as those overnight, part-time jobs rarely turned into full-time positions. The public radio station was where I held one of those weekend jobs. I enjoyed working for them, but I enjoyed the lifelong friendship that ensued even more.

***

While at WCPN, I met and became great friends with Bobby Jackson, who was the program director. God rest his beautiful soul. Bobby and I spent a lot of time together. He took me to jazz concerts that he was reviewing. One time we went to see Wayne Shorter at the Tri-C Jazz Fest. We went backstage after the concert so that Bobby could get an interview. I was meeting a jazz master for the first time in my life. We only exchanged a few pleasantries. Still, it was enough to see how down to earth he was. There was such a peace about him, and no sign of ego anywhere. He spoke to me like we'd known each other our whole lives. The conversation went something like this:

"Hello Maria. It's so nice to meet you. Did you enjoy the concert?" He asked.

"I so enjoyed it. Thank you for your beautiful music Wayne. I'm so inspired." I replied.

"How long have you known Mr. Jackson?" He continued.

"Only briefly," I replied, "I just started working with him at the radio station, but we be came great friends right away."

"Bobby has that effect on people." He said with a chuckle.

Then with wisdom in his voice, Wayne said, "He has a lot of knowledge, you'll be wise to learn from him."

At this point, someone asked him for an autograph. Wayne turned to me and asked,

"Maria, I need a pen, do you have one?" I was giddy the conversation was still going, so I kind of took my time digging around in my purse to find a pen, which I eventually gave him. When he returned it to me, I thought to myself, *"Wayne Shorter used this pen,"* and for several years, I kept it by my keyboard for inspiration and used it to write music. Goodness, what ever happened to that pen? Ha!

Then, I turned around and there was an extremely tall, thin, African American man putting away his electric bass. It was Alphonso Johnson, who was also on the gig. I knew of Alphonso because he also played with Joe Zawinul in Weather Report with Wayne.

Bobby introduced me to Alphonso as a *'hard working and determined vocalist.'* Alphonso must have taken him seriously, because he asked me if I had any CD's that he could hear. He spoke to me like we had been friends for years.

At the time, I only had a demo of what would become part of my first album. I was so tickled that he wanted to hear me sing. I sent it to him, and he responded with a letter. In it, he wrote:

"The music you are working with now will serve you well in any genre you sing. I encourage you to move to LA. I think you could find a lot of work here as a vocalist."

For years, I kept that letter. It also served as inspiration. Goodness, what ever happened to that letter?

I'm afraid that like Wayne's pen, it was a casualty of several unorganized moves and haphazard packing.

***

It was Alphonso who introduced me to the voice teacher who changed my singing life by giving me a real education in vocal technique. Kevyn Lettau is a Brazilian Pop and Jazz vocalist and songwriter. We met upon one of my visits to LA in 1996. I went out one night to meet her and hear her sing at La Ve Lee, a former jazz club in Studio City.

I was blown away. Russell Ferrante, one of my jazz heroes, was on keyboard. We all spoke on a break. Giddy with childlike enthusiasm, I told Kevyn I used to play her recordings as a disc jockey for the Wave and wanted to study with her. She welcomed me and told me to look her up once I made the move.

Between meeting Kevyn and Alphonso, I now had true incentive to finish my debut release and move to LA. *"No Frills"* was a collection of eight favorite standards from the Great American Songbook, and the title track which I wrote. I worked hard to finish the recording so that I could proudly give it to my new friends, colleagues, and teacher.

So many things lined up beautifully as I prepared to move out to the City of Angels. It seemed like it was meant to be. I got a well-paying sales job, pretty much sight unseen. A headhunter found the company, sent them my resume and secured a phone interview. It was a well paying job that I needed desperately and I really pressed the sales manager to hire me. I told him what every employer wants to hear: "I want this job!"

He loved my enthusiasm and fortitude, so he hired me. The company even fronted me my first commission check as moving money. I hadn't even worked a day yet. I was thrilled, and ready to make my move at twenty-nine years of age. Little did I know just how hard the job would be. It served its purpose however, and it got me to LA.

***

For a time, I was incredibly grateful for these new opportunities. The sad fact in all of these seemingly good things, was that I was not walking closely with the Lord. Throughout my successes and failures, I really thought I was doing everything on my own, paying no attention to God. I ignored Him when I was successful, and I ignored Him when I failed, especially during my LA tenure. I believed He existed, I just didn't know how to put Him first, and I suffered tremendously as a result.

I know today that God will let us fail on our own until we learn that it is only through Him that we can succeed. But my failures and struggles were not in vain. Jesus used them all for my good and His glory. This is the reason my Christian testimony exists today. It's the reason I still exist today. I have lived to see another day and to share the miracles that could only come from God, who has always had a plan for my life. This is why *Tell Them About Me,* is less about me, and more about Jesus!

Reflection Points: Things you can do

I think my biggest lesson when I look back on chapter three, relates to how hard I pushed myself. I was so driven to succeed in my profession as a broadcaster as well as a singer. Truth be told, I should have been more willing to slow down and follow my doctors' advice. Before my radio career fell apart, I just refused to take on a nine to five, far more structured routine. I refused to give myself time to breathe. Ironically, I was forced to do just that.

Do you also find yourself in this position? Are you pushing through your struggles, putting your career goals above your health? Are you refusing medication because you don't like how it initially makes you feel?

Yeah, I was there. Looking back, I strongly believe my road might have been less painful had I just taken more time to heal after every setback. In fact, the harder I pushed myself, the greater the setbacks. This was a relentless pattern throughout my life.

I am religious about taking my medication today, but for years, I didn't want to and I allowed myself to be erratic with it. I allowed my hectic schedule to preclude me from taking it regularly. This in fact, was the reason for many of my set-backs.

Career opportunities will always be there, and honestly, we push them farther away when we try to tackle them amidst such intense struggle.

If you find yourself in that place, take a moment now and be still. It's ok to slow down. In fact in doing so, you're probably helping your future career.

Then take out your Jesus Journal, and ask Him to make His plan for your life clear. Go directly to your REAL boss, the One who loves you more than any earthly boss ever could. You are first on His mind.

"Come to me, all you who are weary and burdened, and I will give you rest. Take my yoke upon you and learn from me, for I am gentle and humble in heart, and you will find rest for your souls. For my yoke is easy and my burden is light." - Matthew 11:28-30 NIV

Let Jesus give you rest, the kind that will lead to healing. Give your troubles and struggles to Him, and He will give you strength. I promise, the career will follow. My life is proof of that.

Chapter 4
LA LA Land Wasn't Easy

I was in LA for a total of twelve years, half of which were wonderful, for the most part. While I cannot say I had no struggles early on, working and recording with some of the finest musicians in the world seemed to make up for all of it. Those experiences truly molded, and set me on an upward trajectory musically, and at that point in my life, that was still all I cared about.

While performing in up scale clubs and hotels, I gleaned some wonderful experiences, as well as opportunities to be heard in the jazz community. I opened for Chuck Mangione at the Coach House in San Juan Capistrano, I sang back up for Bobby Kimball (Toto) at B.B. Blues Club, and I sang in LA watering holes where the finest studio musicians hung out and listened. I just did some wonderful things that I could not have done in Cleveland.

As if that weren't enough, I had a contact at Verve Music Group in New York, the head of A&R. I wanted to make another album to submit to him. Alphonso suggested I start with an EP and offered to produce it.

I was thrilled with that idea. We laid out the terms and recorded the first three tracks of my next album, *Chasing Dreams*. He brought Ndugu Chancler in to play drums. Wow, what a dream. Ndugu was responsible for the wide groove you hear when you listen to Michael Jackson's *Billy Jean*, and before that, he played for *Weather Report* with Alphonso. He was not only one of the finest musicians I'd ever worked with, but he was also one of the finest people. He was down to earth and honest. He didn't say much but when he did, it was powerful and usually quite funny. There was also a lovely piano player on those tracks. His name was Geoffrey Aymar.

We recorded Alphonso's arrangements of *"At Last, Lullaby of Birdland"*, and there was also a piano and voice duet of one of my favorite Jimmy McHugh tunes, *"Where Are You?"* We were sure to include its' beautiful but obscure verse that few people ever sang, and to which I felt a strong connection. The song is about losing someone you love and miss terribly. By this point in my life, I could strongly say that I had lived the lyric, the main criteria for singing any song.

With this new EP in my hands, I met with the head of A & R at Verve Music Group in New York. I was staying in New Jersey for the sales training of one of my awful sales jobs and made the drive into the city in the heavy traffic indicative of the concrete jungle. It was worth it.

Though he did not sign me to the label, he was generous with his time and encouraged me to continue on my journey once he heard my music.

He was impressed with this short collection of songs, but unfortunately, Verve had a very full roster of major players. Even with Alphonso Johnson and Ndugu Chancler recording with me, the timing was not right. Still, it was something new to put in my musical treasure chest. I was inspired and hopeful that I might now be on their radar. It fueled me to press on with my dream of becoming a well-established singer, one who made her entire living at her craft.

The next person who heard the EP was Tommy Coster. Tommy was listed in an industry book of all the studios in LA. I called, and as luck would have it, he picked up the phone. This was not a common occurrence in LA. You could almost say, I won a bit of the lottery.

Upon introducing myself, we had a brief conversation. Tommy was open and real. This Multi-Platinum, Grammy Award winning producer and musician co-wrote and co-produced the Real Slim Shady with Eminem and earned a gold record as a teenager for his work with Santana. Let's face it, he didn't have to give me the time of day. After a few minutes on the phone, he asked me an important question.

"Who have you worked with, Maria?"

"I just finished an EP for a forthcoming album with Alphonso Johnson and Ndugu Chancler," I proudly told him.

He was not expecting an answer like that.

"How in the world did you hook up with them?" He asked.

I filled him in on how we met, and it pleased and intrigued him. Tommy and I were friends and colleagues for a long time, but didn't actually work together until I moved back to Cleveland. It was more proof that my tenure in LA was not in vain, and that God was good. LA ended up pounding on me, but in the beginning, there were many good experiences.

I stayed in touch with Tommy over the years, frequently sending him my latest recording efforts. Then one day, in the summer of 2016, he called me. I had been home for seven years.

"Maria, I'd like to write a song with you for my friends Joan Freeman and her husband, Bruce Kessler," Tommy said.

Joan was a very popular and beautiful actress in the 1950's. She was Elvis' leading lady in the movie Roustabout. Without asking why, I simply asked, when?

The song that was Tommy's gift to Joan, became the title track to my sixth album, *Lucky Girl*.

"You're responsible for the melody and the lyrics," Tommy told me. "I'll take care of the rest."

Tommy created the rest of the music to our beautiful song. He assembled some of LA's most talented studio musicians and produced my vocals. We recorded it in his LA studio in the fall of 2016.

The struggles clearly appeared to be worth it, even though this project did not come to fruition until some twenty years later. Relationships and timing are everything. You just never know who you might end up working with one day. This is true in any line of work really, but especially in the music business.

Another telling sign that my years in LA were not just painful, I met and sang with a man who became one of my closest and dearest friends for life. His name is Richard Sherman, and he's a piano player. He remains the dearest man I've ever known, next to my father. We worked together for years. He and his wife Connie literally made me part of the family.

He produced a huge concert every year at the Torrance Civic Center in the South Bay, and every year he included me as a featured artist. This was a benefit concert that he sold out single handedly. He was raising money for Seaside Community Church. I did every concert for more than twenty years, missing only one when I was in treatment in Cleveland. What a gift it was to sing and to be with Richard and Connie. They were a bright spot during some very tough times. Richard also became a mentor to me when it came to my day jobs. He was successful in sales and I was grateful to him for sharing his *'tricks of the trade'* with me. While they did help, I still struggled to hold down many of my account executive positions. The stress levels just were not good for my condition.

***

Working horrible jobs in LA became a relentless pattern. Several of them were sales jobs which involved endless amounts of cold calling all over this unforgiving city.

I used to sell telecom for a GTE and Pac Bell competitor. At one point, the company assigned me the Compton territory. Yes, famous birthplace of Dr. Dre and Kendrick Lamar, but I knew little about it at the time. I mean, they told me it had a high crime rate, but then again, so did East Cleveland, and I'd spent a lot of time there, usually singing. So I really had no fear.

My tall, thin, blonde, runway model of a sales partner and I, walked for hours in business suits, comprised of moderately short skirts, tailored jackets and heels. We probably stood out like sore thumbs. We walked in and out of every office park we could find, seeking small companies whose telephone service we might acquire. We were not real successful on that venture.

It wasn't just the Compton territory, I also hit what seemed like every high rise building in Downtown Los Angeles. Knocking on what seemed like every office door was exhausting. Nearly everyone slammed in my face, and that made it difficult to maintain a positive outlook, which made it equally difficult to ward off depression.

Selling telecom was absolutely brutal. Every closed door brought with it the pressure of falling short of my monthly sales quota. With that came even more stress and the mounting fear of failing to sustain myself financially. Living pretty much hand to mouth, my colleagues and I used to joke about being one paycheck away from homelessness, or worse in my case, sent back to Cleveland.

I eventually left the field of telecom and moved on to the equally stressful job of selling advertising for the LA Weekly, an alternative newspaper with an eclectic staff and client base. This also involved a dreaded amount of cold calling, but on the brighter side, it was a lot more fun.

The sales staff partied together in Hollywood hot spots like the Chateau Marmont, and we had trade deals with some upscale restaurants, where we socialized and dined at no cost.

My favorite one was a high-end seafood restaurant in Beverly Hills, called Crustacean. I loved it there, not only for the $122 Main Lobster that the LA Weekly paid for most of, but also for the five-hundred-gallon fish tank in the floor that gave me vertigo if I dared to look down. It was chic.

My second favorite restaurant was Spago, that everyone who was anyone patronized. I can remember sitting at the bar one night with my visiting sister, just a few seats away from Tony Curtis. We tried not to star gaze, but it was very difficult, especially when moments later, Diana Ross walked in. Yeah, working for the LA Weekly was a gas.

My first client was Larry Flynt, who was opening a new Hustler store on Hollywood Boulevard. I can remember standing outside, looking at scantily clad mannequins in the window, clearly mocking me for my conservative sales clothing. The next thing I knew, a vintage Rolls Royce pulled up with Larry Flynt and his brother inside. His brother had an Ohio State T-shirt on. Both of us alumni, we had an instant conversation starter. He introduced me to Larry. He was friendly, but all about business. The good news is, I got the account. I met my sales quota for the first few months on the Hustler store alone.

I made some friends and a decent living for a while at the LA Weekly. Unfortunately, my health would not remain consistent. The stress was mounting, and I was becoming less and less effective on the job. Between that and some real debacles, like losing a fifteen-hundred-dollar laptop, I was let go. This was the beginning of a revolving door of jobs.

I worked for the Closet Factory for a while, selling and designing elaborate closets for rich people. I sold history books over the phone, then I worked for Michael Ochs Archives, a famous photographer of just about every musical artist you could think of, from Bob Dylan to the Beatles. The pictures were fascinating, but the pay was crap. It sent me waitressing again.

Eventually, I got a great job at the Hertz Corporation. Finally, I had a fantastic account maintenance position that paid well, provided a company car with all its' expenses, and it involved no cold calling. Thank God!

It was fantastic making friends in the office and taking leisurely, two-hour lunches nearly every day. This job was low stress, and I was great at it, maintaining every fortune five hundred company account for which I was responsible, and managing about 100 thousand dollars' worth of their corporate travel. Then a strong dose of reality hit.

Through no fault of my own, my only substantial, stress-free sales job ended in 2001 because of September 11th. They called me into the office one day and told me they had to let good people go because corporate travel was now in significant decline.

I had the largest territory in the office and never missed my sales quota at Hertz. In fact, I was two hundred percent over when corporate headquarters ordered the sales manager to break up my territory among everyone else in the office and let me go. It was the first day job I cried over losing. Devastated and now at a real crossroads, I thought moving back to Cleveland was inevitable. Cue: Richard Sherman, who came to the rescue.

He and Connie invited me to live with them in Torrance until I got back on my feet. He likes to say that it was selfish on his part because he didn't want to lose the singer who performed with his trio regularly. I knew better though. He saw me suffering emotionally, mentally and financially. He wanted to relieve some of my pain, and he did. Their home, and their family, were a welcome oasis in a desert of depression, stress and bipolar cycling.

I did several cream puff gigs with Richard and his trio. Somehow he booked us in places where the food was incredible, and he managed to work meals into our already substantial pay.

We were such typical musicians. We cared more about the food than we did the paycheck. I can remember one place in Redondo Beach, where I ate Osso Bucco every week and drank expensive wine with each meal. That gig didn't last long, I think they just couldn't afford us any longer.

We had an extended stint at the Crowne Plaza Hotel at one point. It remains one of my most treasured memories. I was surrounded by friends on the bandstand, they fed us, (albeit merely hamburgers in the employee cafeteria), and paid us well. I met some incredible people, and the clientele not only listened, they tipped! The music was great, and I grew tremendously as a vocalist.

One of the first friends I made at the Crowne Plaza was Ron Kovic. This was the same Ron Kovic who fought in Vietnam and wrote his autobiography that later became an Oscar win for Tom Cruise. *Born on the Fourth of July* was a brilliant book and movie. Because I knew Ron personally, I could truly appreciate Tom's accurate portrayal of him.

Ron was living in the hotel. What a story he had, which he graciously shared with me. Though we fell out of touch when the gig ended, he was supportive during the few years I knew him. He never stopped encouraging me.

"I know a winner when I see one…you're going to make it," Ron would say.

He even had me hold his Golden Globe over my head like I was accepting it for myself. He called it foreshadowing. He was incredibly sweet, even giving me a copy of his book, which he wrote a personal note in and signed. God bless him. The book and the movie truly honored the man that I knew, and his inscription inspired me. That book and memory I do still have, but he was not the only great person that I met while singing at the Crowne Plaza.

On a Saturday night, one of my jazz singing idols walked in. It was the great Nancy Wilson, with an entourage of friends. I almost fell over. When I began singing "*Who Can I Turn To?*" she actually came up to the bandstand and finished the song with me. We talked during a break, and this is what she said:

"Maria, you should really have them get you some monitors. I could hardly hear myself, and if I can't hear I know you can't hear…what you are doing now you are doing on grace alone…when I can hear myself, I can rip your heart out…so have them get you some monitors if you're going to keep singing with them."

So they did, and I kept singing with them. I can tell you that I am still riding high on these words of encouragement from one of my all time, and greatest musical influences. They were, quite literally, something to write about. Unfortunately, this was in the late nineties, before smart phones. Sadly, no selfies with Nancy.

***

It was while I lived with Richard and Connie that I began writing this book, though at the time, it was really just writing therapy. I never expected to publish it. I was still singing with Richard's trio on weekends, but nowhere else. I was more focused on the written word.

Every morning I got up, made some tea, lit some candles, and wrote for hours. My writing therapy chronicled every pitfall I could call to mind, but after only a few months I had to put the book down. It was a difficult time, and while writing was cathartic, it just became too much to relive.

Once stronger, I moved out to live in a beautiful house in Santa Monica, close to my cousins and Godfather on the Jacobs side of my family. My roommates, once again, were two very good male friends and what turned out to be their girlfriends as well. They were actors. I stay in touch with both guys to this day. One of them is Lebanese. Brian and I still call each other '*cousin.*'

He convinced me to go to an acting school he was in, and spoke of highly. I attended for little over a year. While it did whet my appetite to peak into the actress and writer side of myself, in the long run, it wasn't a good fit. The details of why are really beyond the scope of this book, but the crux of the impasse we came to, was the fact that they, like many other groups of people in my life at the time, wanted me off of my medication. They didn't believe I needed it and intimated I was weak for taking it. It was extremely out of bounds. The director chose to call me out on it during his acting critique in front of everyone. Ugh!

These anti-medication people put a lot of pressure on me. They were adamantly against it and wasted no time telling me so. It was deeply hurtful as I was truly vulnerable in this area. While I knew to separate myself from them, their toxic energy seemed to follow me. I knew from experience how important my treatment was, but all of that negativity left a kind of emotional residue on me. I began to self-doubt and question myself,

"Do I really need the medication? Could they be right about it? Am I weak for needing it? Do I need to get off of it in order to have a career?

Yeah, they got to me. After all, I would have loved it if I wasn't on medication. Let's face it, nobody really wants to be, at least that's what I told myself.

When I told my family I didn't want to take medication anymore, each one of them painfully reminded me of how bad it was years prior. It was a reality I didn't want to face. I wanted to believe I was so much stronger now and I would be fine without it. I wanted to believe those negative people were actually right, but deep down I knew they weren't.

Still, I went back and forth, one minute believing the meds were necessary to live a normal life, and the next minute planning how I would ween myself off of them. I essentially had emotional whiplash.

I didn't know who I should listen to and it was painful. Eventually however, my common sense won out. I finally just chalked the naysayers up to being ignorant and irresponsible. It was my family who helped me to see that, a family that they even urged me to leave for what they called lack of support. They were so wrong.

***

Writing a book about your life experiences is not easy, at least not for me. I find myself wanting to tell my story without being disparaging to anyone. It's a bit of a tightrope walk at times, but to be effective, a writer has to be transparent, authentic, and a little bit vulnerable.

Yes, I was too open about being bipolar. It was a mistake I made repeatedly out there, because this was long before I stabilized and became the advocate that I am today. I became a bit of a target to several groups of people around whom I would find myself.

Since we all play a role in the things that happen to us, I have to admit I invited a good deal of the discrimination and criticism I endured. Still, it was difficult to keep it all to myself. I was looking for support and understanding in all the wrong places. The painful result of which, was more isolation and emotional turmoil.

Surprisingly, I went on to find a much better acting environment, as I couldn't shake the desire I had to continue to explore this side of my creative self. It was a workshop where we read for casting directors. It was a relief, and I enjoyed it, though I was still mood cycling between depression and mania and trying hard to navigate through the intrusive thoughts that swarmed my head. The most relentless one was the belief that those medication naysayers were still targeting me. Deep down I knew that *probably* wasn't the case, but it was still a recurring thought I couldn't shake. You can expect a lot of disordered thoughts like these while dealing with bipolar disorder.

Intellectually I knew they were not real, or at the very least, could not be proven. Still they were so painful, difficult to ignore, and they caused sleepless nights filled with anxiety for a long time. That is, until I learned to lean strongly on God's word, which tells us explicitly how to handle them.

"Be strong; fear not! Behold, your God will come with vengeance, with the recompense of God. He will come and save you."
—- Isaiah 35:4 ESV

"Do not be anxious about anything, but in everything by prayer and supplication with thanksgiving, let your request be made known to God, and the peace of God which surpasses all understanding will guard your hearts and mind in Christ Jesus"
—- Philippians 4:6-8 ESV

Despite these difficulties, I was enjoying this new class. I was surrounded by actors who were finding work in Hollywood. They had acting credits on their resumes. Mine had some radio work and a lot of singing gigs. I learned a lot, but I was not booking acting jobs.

Tell Them About Me

While I was there, I made another great friend who helped me along the way. Still mood cycling, I could no longer go to class, so she took me on as my one-on-one acting coach. Mostly, she was using art to help me communicate and heal. She never even charged me. She later designed my website and a few of my album covers. She didn't charge me for that either. I owe a great deal to Jody, one of the few people who didn't discriminate, pressure me, or back off because I was clearly in poor health. God bless her, she pulled me closer. In addition, she was honest with me, no sugar coating about the business. I truly appreciated that. We are friends to this day, and I so appreciate that as well.

Honestly, the chronology of everything that happened next is a total blur. I moved around a lot, I job hopped, and I drank too much. In fact, you could say this was the part of my bipolar disorder that everyone warned me about.

Drinking was not an issue in Cleveland, but as things worsened across the board in LA, so did my alcohol intake. For several years I mistakenly self-medicated hoping to numb the pain, drinking alone most of the time. I was impaired by depression and mania, which was getting worse. I began reaching for alcohol when I was angry and depressed, and that was an awful combination. I wasn't merely sipping wine socially anymore, now I was abusing alcohol and my condition worsened.

I can remember one rainy morning I was headed up the 405 freeway from Redondo Beach. I was on my way to see my doctor at a mental health facility for people who had very little money and no insurance. All I can say is, I got what I paid for. Up until then I was receiving treatment at

Cedar Sinai Medical Hospital, but I could no longer afford it because I no longer had a full-time job, or benefits.

On the way there, I was on the phone calling bill collectors asking them for payment plans rather than the whole lump sum that I owed. They were mostly credit card companies, and they were refusing, demanding all of their money right away. I just didn't have it. I was living on credit cards because I had no money and I was in collections all over the place.

All I can remember is how rude and condescending they were, offering no assistance whatsoever. I became angry and irritated in addition to being desperate and depressed. To make matters worse, I received the same disrespectful treatment when I arrived at the facility.

I checked in at the front desk with people who obviously did not like their part-time jobs. Hearing how rude they were to other outpatients unnerved me. When it was my turn, they were rude to me as well.

If I remember correctly, they did not have me down as having an appointment that day. I was certain that I did, and I was adamant that I see my doctor. They were not compassionate. I really did my best to be diplomatic at first but they made it very hard. The more I insisted, the more disrespectful they became.

I finally got in to see my doctor. It's important to note, that while I was in treatment with her, she made a habit of putting me on a drug and then sending me on my way with no follow up whatsoever. She never answered my calls if I reached out to her while having a hard time.

At first, I tried respectfully to let her know I was unhappy with my treatment and felt very neglected. Displeased with me, she then became rude and disrespectful too, as if I didn't matter at all. Let's face it, to her I didn't. I was just a number. This made me angry, and we ended up arguing. She screamed at me for pressing her and for arguing with the front desk, deflecting the attention away from her own neglect.

As for the help I was looking for regarding my medication, it never came. She simply barked at me to be compliant with what she prescribed, and she paid no attention to what I was telling her about my symptoms. I was struggling. I knew something was not right and wanted her to prescribe something different, but she would not.

I left in tears. I was in a depressed state and I didn't know what I was doing. I was completely impaired. The place I went to for help was not helpful. On the contrary, the people there were harmful. It is obvious to me now how so many fall through the cracks.

Driving recklessly, I went speeding home while entertaining the most severe suicidal thoughts I had ever remembered. I just believed that my life was worthless, and didn't feel I could turn to my family. They had seen me go through so much already. I didn't want them to see that I was mood cycling yet again, so I isolated.

I went to a liquor store and bought a bottle of wine. I took it home, sat on my bed and cried while drinking alone. It was the first time to date that I could remember taking a drink amidst so much intense anger and depression.

When I stopped drinking, I went into the bathroom, and in a fit of anger, I smashed the bottle over the sink. With glass and wine everywhere, I sat on the floor and sobbed, wondering how God could allow me to fall into this dark place. It was another test of my faith, and I was failing.

Ironically, I did not have much wine, maybe just one or two glasses. I know because most of it was all over my bathroom floor. It was not the volume of consumption that concerned me, however. It was the fact that I reached for a drink out of intense anger, and it made me feel out of control. I had self-medicated before, but drinking under these circumstances was even scarier than previous episodes. I put alcohol on top of depression, despair and anger combined, and that was a dangerous combination which frightened me.

I did the right thing though, I stopped drinking for years, three to be exact, but I needed help to do it. I went where people go to stop drinking, the program. Ironically, I sought out the inpatient treatment I spoke of earlier at my one year, and at my eighteen-month, sober mile marker. It was proof that it wasn't all about alcohol. My disease was kicking me hard, ironically, even more so while I was sober. I just could not get it together.

It wasn't only the drinking I tortured myself with, I also struggled tremendously with food. Food was actually my first drug. Before I began self-medicating with alcohol, I was doing so with food. There were some days I'd stay in bed all day, even in my early years in LA, feeling depressed, and binging on cheese and junk food from a nearby 7-eleven. There were struggles out there long before I hit rock bottom.

It was also not uncommon for me to get up at two a.m., and drive to that all night store to buy those Friday's restaurant appetizers, like potato skins, jalapeño poppers, mozzarella sticks and chicken wings. I'd come home and cook them in the middle of the night and binge.

Between my bad eating habits and the medication that I was on, I really struggled with my weight, which brought on so much insecurity and self-loathing. I had an extra thirty pounds on me for a very l long time and it was so hard to lose it and keep it off for long. I yo-yo'd up and down for years.

Honestly, if I am to choose which struggle was worse, alcohol or food, I'd have to say it was the food, because that has gone on for a lifetime, really. I was and am an emotional eater who was born with bad eating habits. I had them even as a child.

I can remember at seven or eight years old, getting up early, ahead of the rest of my family on some Saturday mornings. I would watch television and help myself to anything in the kitchen. There was no one there to tell me "*don't eat that,*" so I thought I was really getting away with something. My food choices, however, were cause for concern. I just didn't know any better.

I used to go to the cupboard and eat Bisquick, and brown sugar to my heart's content, and follow it up with potato chips that came in a two-foot tall can that we kept in the corner of our kitchen. What could possibly make my heart content with food choices like this is beyond me, but I did not get honest about my eating until I got much older.

I managed my struggle with alcohol, which lasted only a couple of years, but if I'm being completely honest, I still struggle with my food, making it difficult to sustain my ideal weight. The meds are lifesaving, but I'm afraid weight gain just comes with the territory. They slow down one's metabolism, and it becomes extremely hard to burn off what I eat. I went completely dry from alcohol for years, but I still had to eat and when I did, it was not always in a healthy manner.

***

Many of the people I met while getting sober were other sober musicians who invited me to sing with them. We played a lot of sober parties, and this made me happy in the midst of a lot of turmoil. Once again, music was proving to be great therapy.

Some of the friendships were dysfunctional as hell. We were all struggling. I had a sponsor who was supposed to be leading me down a road to sobriety, but she collapsed one day out of nowhere and was immediately diagnosed with multiple sclerosis. She could barely walk anymore and I ended up caring for her and being there for her, rather than the other way around. I mean it was good to be of service, but I was left without a solid sponsor who could help me at the time I needed it the most.

These friendships eventually waned over the years. This was with the exception of one girlfriend who let me live with her for a while. I was on the fence about staying in LA or returning home. Kelly was supportive. I knew I really didn't want to go back to Cleveland, so I helped her watch her kids and straighten her house. You know, I tried to make myself useful in exchange for a place to live. I just couldn't go back home while things were so terrible. I wanted to return a success, but I was a far cry from being one.

Eventually, a good friend saw that my life and treatment wasn't going well and he referred me to a great therapist. This doctor didn't mess around. When she saw my condition, she wasted no time and got the paperwork started to put me on disability. She wanted me focusing on my health and not the stressful, full-time jobs I was invariably fired from over and over again.

Though I needed the assistance, I felt I had hit an all-time low. Then things got a little bit better. I got this job teaching music part-time at a Catholic School, St. Joseph School in Hawthorne, California. It was an urban, predominantly Hispanic population. While it was my dear friend Richard who secured that interview for me, let's face facts, that job was a perfect example of God showing up. He works through the people He places in our lives. Clearly, He wanted me back in church. I not only taught in the classroom, I also cantored the Mass regularly, and it was good for me. At this difficult time, God was what I needed. So I guess you could say that this job was a bit of a miracle.

Teaching there was enjoyable. In fact, it was the first time I thought that a full-time teaching career might be in my future. Nearly two years flew by before more trouble hit. That was when I had to leave for inpatient treatment for what ended up being twice in six months.

I was pushing myself too hard once again. While teaching at St. Joseph School, I was also going back to school in Orange County to try and become a Music Therapist. A friend of mine put a bug in my ear that this too could be a future profession for me. Once again, I was trying to do it all, desperate to make some kind of success of myself. I was trying to secure my future, which was looking very unstable.

Mistakenly believing that it was safe to reveal my condition in this music therapy environment, I told the department head of my documented disability. The only thing he was required to do, was provide me with the accommodation of extra test taking time. When it came to scheduling observation sites, or helping when they were unorganized; being lenient with assignment deadlines, or just being accepting regarding my condition and the fact that I was on medication, he was of no help whatsoever. He was basically compassionless on every other level.

For example, those observation sites where we had to work for our required field experience, were basically unpaid, part-time jobs and they were time consuming. I worked with the whole spectrum of children and adults with Autism, the elderly, and emotionally disturbed adults and children, many of whom were violent. It was the hardest work I had ever done. I had a hard time juggling those jobs with a full class load while also teaching music part-time. To make matters worse, this educational experience did not end well.

When one of the sites cancelled my first six hours of observation due to their own mismanagement, he was of no assistance in getting them back on track. When I turned around and missed one more hour to go out of town for the weekend, all hell broke loose.

Following that, the head of the department came down very hard on me. He knew I had been in treatment. He was no fan of medication, as he made it abundantly clear in class while talking about mood disorders like manic depression. He believed music therapy was the only answer. I knew how powerful music was and I couldn't imagine my life without it, but I'd be dead without medication.

When I missed that last hour of observation, he kicked me out of the program, and he was very disrespectful and unprofessional about it. He and the adjunct professor of the department called me into his office, and she began speaking to me sarcastically and diminutively, as though I were a second grader. All the while, he sat in the corner smirking and sending condescending vibes through facial expressions and emotionally intimidating body language.

I was so angry and hurt I could literally feel my body temperature rise and my stomach was in knots. I suppressed my anger because I knew if I lost my temper, it would just fuel their fire. Afterall, I didn't want to give them real reason to kick me out of the program, since the first was flimsy at best. It felt like they were intentionally trying to make me feel bad.

I fought for myself a little bit, but the fix was in. It was two against one, no witnesses and no advocates. There was nothing I could do about it. Three years of my music therapy degree program that I worked so incredibly hard at, were going down the drain.

The department head knew what I was going through. He knew that most of the observation cancellations were not my fault, but he still removed me from the program. It was discrimination that I could not prove. I complained to the president of the school, putting everything in writing. I can still remember our telephone conversation following his receipt of my letter.

"Miss Jacobs, why would he discriminate against someone with a disability? He's a music therapist; it makes no sense!"

I replied by verbally reinforcing what I put in that letter.

"You should hear him talk in class when the subject of medication comes up for people with bipolar disorder or other mental illness. He doesn't believe in it. He thinks music therapy is the only answer."

Still, he publicly supported his colleague. My hopes that he would be fired over this, were dashed.

While the president of the school obviously did not admit to discrimination, he did expunge my record and to me, this was very telling. I can't say for sure if that department head was ever reprimanded, but I did see him walking across campus shortly after this all went down. His body language indicated that he must have endured some sort of consequence. That's what I wanted to believe anyway. He was walking slowly into the music building with his head hanging very low, and with a look of extreme sadness on his face. Here's hoping he at least got a stern talking to. Here's hoping the president of the school was as condescending to him as he was to me. Well, that's what I told myself anyway.

Right or wrong, the thought of it made me feel a little better. I was unable to fight all of this, but I was determined to move on to another program. At this point in my life, I truly believed I would one day become a Music Therapist. In addition to that however, I was damned if I was going to let them win. This situation and these people, became a lesson in how to overcome unforgiveness issues, which mounted for years.

***

After being removed from that school in Orange County, which shall remain nameless, I moved from Redondo Beach to North Hollywood and enrolled at Cal State Northridge, which had a wonderful Music Therapy Program. I was still teaching at St. Joseph School in Hawthorne. I spoke of this a bit in a previous chapter.

Remember, I left there temporarily after about a year, to enter my first inpatient treatment. I was awake for four days straight with extreme mania, paranoid, fearful and dropping weight rapidly. After a week in that moderately successful treatment program, the principal was gracious enough to let me return to my position of music instructor. I was so grateful to her for that.

So, there I was going to school full-time again, this time in Northridge, and driving to Hawthorne three times a week to teach. You'd have to know LA really well to understand how geographically ridiculous it was to do this. I drove nearly two hours in LA traffic from one location to the other. I was trying to do it all, desperate to make a success out of myself. It was just too much stress. I missed my medication frequently, and that's when extreme mania hit again. I mean it was the definition of insanity. I was doing the same thing over and over and expecting different results that I would not achieve.

This is what led to that second inpatient treatment in six months, and nearly another four days with no sleep. It was so painful to go through it again, and to make matters worse, I had to leave another music therapy program for a second time, this time voluntarily. It seemed I could do nothing right. I had to leave a job I loved for the second time, and another Music Therapy program. The City of Angels was hitting harder and harder.

My family all begged me to return home but I just couldn't do it. I was not ready to cash in my chips. Can you believe it? I felt strongly that once I left LA I would be kissing any hopes of a music career goodbye. I still wanted a career more than I wanted God, more than I wanted my health, and a lot more than I wanted to surrender it all to Him. I was filled with self-will, and it was killing me slowly.

After both inpatient treatments, I did return home for five months to receive outpatient treatment at the Cleveland Clinic. I was not happy about it. I didn't know at the time if I would ever get back to LA and that saddened me terribly. I had no job and no money other than the modest disability checks every month, so I lived with my parents again. I loved them, but I wanted my independence, and it was nowhere in sight. To lighten the load a bit, I auditioned for a musical in one of the community theaters in the area.

I'll never forget the fun I had doing *I Love You, You're Perfect, Now Change* at Western Reserve Playhouse. It was there that I met my future (ex) husband, who was also in the four-person cast. I fully believe this man was meant to be in my life, and if I am being completely honest, I grew tremendously while we were together, but I'm afraid we were not meant to last.

I left him after six years of marriage, but we were together for a total of twelve. Among other tremendous issues between us, we were unequally yoked, and it came out in many significant ways. I believe my marriage to him was allowed by God, I do not believe it was ordained by God. Still, he played a significant role in my life. God can work through anyone and anything; everyone and everything. He drew me closer to Him through many of my missteps, even an unequally yoked marriage. This is why *Tell Them About Me*, is less about me, and more Jesus!

Reflection Points: Things you can do

Take a moment now and think about what you've just read. By now, you might be asking yourself:

"Did she stumble because her disease cycled, or because she took her eyes off of Christ?"

Excellent. I have asked myself this question over and over again, once healthy. The answer is, both. The truth is, yes, I did take my eyes Christ, for years, and He let me fail repeatedly for years, until I learned the hard way that I was not made to handle things on my own. On the contrary, we are all made to be dependent on God.

"I am the vine; you are the branches. If you remain in me and I in you, you will bear much fruit: apart from me you can do nothing."
—- John 15:5

Apart from Jesus, I truly did nothing!

You just read a pretty harrowing chapter, right? With all of that, I could have been lost forever, but God would not have it. He knew where He would ultimately lead me. Why did I have to sink so far down before turning my life over to Him? One part disease, two parts self-will. Boy was I stubborn. What I do know, is that I am grateful for every hardship that drew me closer to Christ, even if it took many years to get there. What a testimony I have as a result. A testimony as to how Jesus changed the course of my life.

"Not only so, but we also glory in our sufferings, because we know that suffering produces perseverance; perseverance, character; and

character, hope. *And hope does not put us to shame, because God's love has been poured out in our hearts through the Holy Spirit, Who has been given to us."* —— Romans 5:3-5 NIV

Take a moment now and sit quietly with God. Then, take out your Jesus Journal and write down some of those tiny steps you can take towards Him. Don't make it difficult. It could just mean beginning your day with a prayer, maybe the Lord's Prayer. It could also mean beginning your day with a Scripture. Maybe it just means asking God to make your next steps clear, or better yet, simply turning your next steps over to Jesus. Literally put that in your Jesus journal. Try it…just for today.

If this is new to you, you will soon be surprised. What starts out with *"just for today,"* will soon become today and tomorrow. Before you know it, you'll be turning your life over to God. Will that make it perfect? No, I'm not going to lie. God never promised days without pain. He did, however, give us His Word that He would never leave us. I don't know about you, but that makes my *'heavy'* days, a lot lighter.

"Even to your old age and gray hairs I am He, I am He who will sustain you, I have made you and I will carry you; I will sustain you and I will rescue you." — Isaiah 46:4 NIV

Chapter 5
Chasing Dreams All The Way Home

I don't want to identify my ex-husband, so I'm going to change his name. Eric and I really liked each other from the start, but he was involved with someone. We did nothing about our crush on each other the entire time we were working together those five months I was home. My outpatient treatment was going well and I was doing a lot better. Since it seemed at the time that nothing would happen between us, I returned to LA once the play closed. No one thought it was a good idea, but I didn't listen. My self-will was still in overdrive.

I managed to find roommates again, renting rooms in their beautiful houses, but still never really feeling at home anywhere I went. I tried several part-time jobs while I collected disability. I have to admit, as much as I hated being on government assistance, it helped tremendously since I could not consistently hold down full-time work.

Then one day, I got an email from Eric, asking if I would be home for Christmas. When I said yes, he asked me to dinner. He had broken up with his girlfriend and wanted to spend some time together. I was elated.

I visited home for the holidays, and we went on our first date in December of 2007. We were together from that point on. I was still a resident of LA at the time, so we continued to date long distance.

One of the compassionate things about Eric was, he learned early on about my conditions, and he never judged me. At the time, this was all I wanted from a partner. Everyone else in LA was quite the opposite. I truly believed God had sent him. When I told him I was bipolar, he took the time to actually do research so that he could understand me better. He saw me through an episode while we were dating long distance. This was the third big one in one year, though this time I narrowly escaped inpatient treatment.

It was in the fall of 2008. Eric and I were in the middle of our long-distance relationship. I'll never forget it. I was living in a ritzy apartment building, Sterling International Towers, right at the corner of Wilshire and Beverly Glen. I was the roommate of a woman who owned her own wig business and had alopecia also. She gave me a job. Having alopecia myself, we both thought it was a great fit.

I knew living with someone I worked for could turn out to be a disaster, but I needed a job and a place to live. I took her up on her invitation to be her roommate. Everything was great at first. There was even a pool on the roof and the apartments were gorgeous.

That's when the third cycle in 2008 hit. I have to tell you, there was nothing violent about me when episodic. What you could expect from me were some run on sentences that didn't always make sense. Reality testing issues surfaced again. She could see that I wasn't myself on the job, unable to concentrate and therefore not real effective. My job entailed some light administrative work, but my pace was very slow. In addition, she had me help her redecorate her office, a job I really botched. I pained the walls a bright yellow without covering the furniture and virtually ruined a nice leather couch because I didn't cover it first. She was livid, and fired me.

It's hard for me to remember what came next. All I know is that she was now being made privy to what mania entailed. She swears to this day that we had a heated argument and that's when I told her I had to fix my meds.

"Meds? What the hell are you talking about?" She asked me, with her arms around me to keep me calm.

"I'm bipolar" I told her.

"What the hell is 'bipolar?'"

I explained as best I could, with broken sentences, and a broken heart. I just couldn't believe this was happening again.

I wish I could remember more. What I do painfully remember, is her asking me to move out of the apartment. I had nowhere to go, but that was of no consequence to her. She felt she had to remove me. Yes, it was a bad idea to live with my boss.

Facing the homelessness I used to joke about, it was a great drummer friend of mine to the rescue. Frankie listened to me crying on the phone that I was in trouble. Living with my LA family wasn't an option. I just couldn't tell them how bad it was getting. Not only was I embarrassed, I knew they didn't believe that I should stay in LA. They thought it best if I returned to Cleveland, which I was still not ready to do. I thought I had to handle this without my family, and sadly, without God, who was clearly telling me to get the hell out of LA. Once again, my self-will would not have it.

Frankie came over that night and helped me pack up everything. I had very little since I took only the bare necessities when I left Cleveland following those five months of outpatient treatment. He let me stay with him in his run down guest house in Beverly Hills until I could get back on my feet. The house attached to it must have been the only one on the street that hadn't had multi-million-dollar renovations. It wasn't glamorous. I slept on a little air mattress on the floor. It had a hole in it and it kept deflating. It was not comfortable, but who was I to complain? I had a place to stay, and it kept me out of Cleveland.

Every morning I got up and went for a walk. I'm telling you, the houses that were glamorous, were really glamorous. Every other one had a pastel-colored Bentley in the driveway.

LA is the place of the haves and the have-nots. I don't have to tell you which one I was. This was never more evident than while I was staying with Frankie. I did find another place fairly soon. In fact, I returned to North Hollywood.

At this time, Eric was kicking around the idea of moving there so that we could be closer. That's when it hit me.

Am I really happy here? I asked myself. The answer was no, no I wasn't. So I told Eric, "I just don't think I can stay here any longer."

With that, I decided it was time to leave LA, forever.

***

Eric and I were serious now. I dated a bit in LA, but never to the extent of a serious relationship. In fact, Eric was my first serious relationship since my first boyfriend at

18 years old. Dating while living with bipolar disorder was difficult, and I lived with it my entire adult life.

It was particularly difficult to have a serious relationship while in the City of Angels. Nearly everyone out there is a transient, commitment-phobe. In addition, focusing on the development of a music career while often struggling, left little time to pursue anything serious.

Most of the people in LA were not as compassionate as Eric. I lack the time, and the inclination to tell you how many 'friends' left my life because they just couldn't handle what I was experiencing. Though I listened to all of their stories on a regular basis, no one wanted to hear about bipolar disorder. I guess it still had a stigma attached to it.

Looking back, I can see that I was a handful, talking about my condition as often as I did. Beyond that, my heart was in the right place. Sadly however, it was crushed over and over again in an endless cycle of unrequited love and fair-weather friends. Deeply hurtful gossip found its way back to me along with trash talk about my needy, run on sentences and admittedly relentless phone calls at times. I tried too hard to connect with people whom I knew were judging me for all of the above, and whom I knew just wanted me out of their lives. My apologies didn't even seem to matter to them.

The more I knew it, the harder I tried. I guess I was a little scrappy. I wanted to fix what I knew was broken in my relationships, but let's face it, everyone involved must want the same thing for that to work, and they didn't.

Later, I had to remind myself that God removes people from your life if He sees that they are no longer good for you. It's painful to lose those you care for, but once I became grateful, really and truly grateful to God, I no longer focused on those I lost, but rather, the love of those that remained. They became fewer, but truer.

I left LA in February of 2009, this time for good. While back in my hometown of Cleveland, I had a real home for the first time, a home cultivated with my new boyfriend who truly cared about me.

The first night in our new apartment was the best sleep I had in years. I finally belonged somewhere. After all of the horrendous turmoil throughout the last twelve years, I finally had some peace, though it was often times accompanied by the realization I may never have the career I dreamt about. I learned to be at peace with that as well.

Though it would be a while before I would fully return to my Catholic faith, I did become closer to God, thanking Him for everything. How could I not? Look at what He did for me, bringing me through some pretty rocky waters. I thanked Him when life was going well, and I thanked Him when it wasn't. This became a huge turning point in my life.

***

Life continued to evolve. Eric and I found an Italian restaurant up the street that we patronized frequently. It became our second home where everyone, staff and customers, knew us. He was also part of the thriving theater community in the surrounding areas. It was filled with a large group of artists who welcomed me as their friend. I had a life. Consequently, my new living stability made it possible for my music to grow little by little and I began to do more music writing.

I went back to school at Kent State University at 40 years old. I was now getting a second degree, this time in music education with a minor in education. I was singing a fair amount but Cleveland was not yet a place where musicians had ample venues to play, especially to play jazz. I began performing in New York whenever I could. I put a band together in town that invariably folded after a year or two.

I found a promoter through my distributor whom I met at an LA industry workshop, but who lived in Cleveland. He was another one of the many reasons that I know my life in LA was not completely fruitless, despite its ups and downs.

I was starting to get some national radio airplay with a song I wrote called *Pour Me a Cup of Yesterday*. I was beginning to have some upward mobility over and above Cleveland, but the radio promotions were expensive and I did not have enough financial backing to continue with them. In fact, I was lucky that my guitar player at the time, believed in me enough to buy the proverbial lottery ticket and financially backed the radio promotion.

Jim was in my band '*4Get the Girl,*' named cleverly because it consisted of four guys and me. We had some great times together. We played Playhouse Square and some other sweet gigs around town. We even made a decent EP of three of my original tunes. We rehearsed regularly for a while, until it was clear we just weren't working enough. Incentive for rehearsing was waning on them. While Jim and I were on the same page as far as rehearsing more, the others just could not do it with so few gigs in sight. The timing was just not right anymore, so I pulled the plug on the band.

Pour Me A Cup Of Yesterday did well however, and Jim never regretted the financial backing. It charted on the Groove Jazz Charts. It was played a lot on Cleveland's Wave

Station, 107.3. They really supported Cleveland based artists and their projects. For me, it all meant my first royalty payment from ASCAP, and a lot more visibility as an artist.

***

God was really turning out in my life. The road I walked to arrive at this point was surely not easy. Personally and spiritually, it did bend and turn, but I eventually found my way home. Eric did make a difficult road much easier for a time, and for that I will always be grateful to him.

Our marriage ended for many reasons. In short, I was so focused on his acceptance of my condition, that I overlooked some important differences with which I could no longer live. Suffice it to say, we had some major communication issues, and as I said, we were unequally yoked. I'm going to respect his privacy on the rest.

In truth, I was also not as devout in my faith when we met. In that regard, I was the one who changed. He was not a believer, and as much as I eventually wanted to share my faith with my husband, I couldn't.

We did not have a Catholic marriage. He did not want one. We were married by a Protestant minister who was a friend of ours. Having not had a Catholic wedding made getting an annulment from the Catholic Church much easier. I quite literally had one within ten days of receiving my divorce decree. If God sees fit to let me marry again, it will be under His perfect will for my life, not merely His permissive will, and it will be a Sacramental marriage.

True, we lived together before we married, but that didn't help our marriage. It was a mistake I won't make again. What I will say is, God is merciful. He once again carried me through one of life's most difficult times. He was faithful to me, even when I was not faithful to Him.

I left my husband in 2020. Like all of us, I was navigating through the rough terrain of living in the Covid pandemic. I was reinventing the wheel as a virtual teacher, going through a divorce, getting an annulment, selling our home and moving into a single apartment, and living alone again for the first time in over a decade. As if that weren't enough, I was also helping to care for my mother who was in a severe dementia decline. Seriously, I could write an entire book based on 2020 alone, but Jesus was there through it all. He never left my side, and I was beginning to awaken to this fact.

He was now filling my life with more friends and a faith community that became lifesaving. My spiritual life was blooming like a rose in the desert. That is just how God works, and this is why *Tell Them About Me*, is less about me, and more about Jesus.

Reflection Points: Things you can do

There is a very important take-away in chapter five. I finally came to a place of acceptance. For me, that meant leaving Los Angeles, the place where I was convinced I would make a way for myself. It was the place where I thought my life and my career would take off, but God had other plans.

Let me ask you, are you in a place in your life right now where you too have to come to a place of acceptance, or are you *'white knuckled,'* so to speak? Are you refusing to let go of a place, a person, a job, a group of friends, that you need to let go of, but maybe you are afraid of doing so? I get it. I was there.

Letting go of a place was hard, but letting go of people? Wow did that hurt. God did for me what I couldn't do for myself. He removed some people who were no longer right for me, but in His infinite Grace and Mercy, He eventually replaced them with those who truly enriched my life and blessed me. I did not look forward to replacing LA with Cleveland, but as you read, God's plan turned out to be much better than mine.

Take a moment now and ask God what or whom He may be telling you to step away from. Take a moment and ask Him where in your life you need to come to a place of acceptance. I know how hard it is to let go of people, places and things to which you've grown attached. Maybe God feels you have outgrown them, or more importantly, maybe He feels you *need* to outgrow them. When I finally let go of my will and trusted God's, I learned why we pray, "…

Thy will be done on Earth as it is in Heaven." In my acceptance of His will, He changed my life, and His Divine Providence took over, lifting me to a higher calling, one that allowed me to fulfill my dreams, all while glorifying Him in the process. What a mighty God we serve!

Are you still having trouble believing that God can do that? Take out your Jesus Journal and make a list of those people, places and things your gut is telling you no longer fit your life. Ask God to reveal to you exactly what or whom you may just need to remove from your life right now.

In this place of acceptance, that disruptive anxiety you've grown accustomed to will be replaced by peace that could only come from God, and you too will become Grateful. I am a witness!

> *"Cast all your anxiety on Him because He cares for you."*
> *—- 1 Peter 5:7 NIV*

Chapter 6
The Crooked Lines That Led Me Back To Faith

Experiencing depression, mania, and suicidal ideation, can leave you depleted in every way. A once balanced mental, emotional and spiritual life, was thrown off kilter. Being alone with it all was excruciating, but Jesus was there, providing much needed strength. It is so obvious now why there was only one set of footprints in the sand for years, as the allegorical poem describes. Then a good friend reminded me of a popular proverb.

"God writes straight with crooked lines."

This made so much sense, especially when it came to faith. Jesus was always there, but the walk with Him was rarely a straight line, bouncing between jobs, schools, living environments, roommates and even churches. Often, taking long absences from organized religion altogether, meant that worship was not a priority. Knowing that God existed did not change the fact that bipolar disorder was taking a wrecking ball to a once rich faith life, telling the lie that God just wasn't listening.

The Catholic Mass became painful and difficult to celebrate, even in the Eastern Rite where I'd spent most of my life. The disease and its symptoms crept into the Roman Catholic Mass as well, causing tears and more painful reminders that church no longer felt like home.

Listening to fellow parishioners pray aloud and sing hymns, all triggered negative emotions and a sick emptiness that was heartbreaking. So many questions penetrated a mind impaired by depression and mania:

"Why was God allowing me to suffer so much hurt? Why don't I feel at home in the Catholic Church anymore? Why could I no longer feel the Holy Spirit? Where did I belong spiritually?"

The answers were not clear, and it led to church shopping while living in LA, observing and singing in the choir of an Episcopalian Church, and then singing in a Gospel/Jazz choir in a church of religious science. That was followed by chanting and meditating with some Buddhist friends. They insisted it would allow for relaxation and help return this troubled soul to a peaceful sleep, of which mania had robbed her. Sadly, it didn't. On the contrary, it all left nothing but more feelings of emptiness. All the pain, the sadness, trauma and yes, the ghosts and demons from the past, were relentless. Blaming these surroundings, I ran from them.

There were just too many emotional issues looming, including the breakup with an abusive ex-boyfriend who ridiculed faith and family. There were also the repeated mood cycles and disordered, intrusive thoughts that never seemed to rest. It also didn't help that the loss of a once idyllic life could still be credited to the onset of bipolar disorder.

Those crooked lines were painful, but God is merciful. He does not want pain to be in vain, so He sends lessons along the way, lessons that would make these paths straight in time.

"Trust in the Lord with all your heart, And lean not on our own understanding. In all your ways acknowledge Him, And He will make your paths straight." —- *Proverbs 3:5-6 NIV*

That was the biggest lesson, but it took a long time and a very profound, supernatural experience with Jesus before it would become clear. It's the one that made this book a Christian testimony, rather than simply a memoir.

Just know that as with all mysteries of the Christian Faith, this supernatural experience is and always will remain a beautiful mystery as well.

Some Christians, throughout the course of conversation, end their sentenced with the words, "The Lord told me!" This begged some questions:

"Did you actually hear His Voice? What did He sound like?"

For some, this is a common occurrence and nothing new. Friends in a Charismatic, Non-Denominational Church spoke of it freely and often, but this was unfamiliar before that dark, dark day. Though God's timing will cause disbelief in the minds of some readers, others will accept it, rejoice and know that His timing was perfect, as it always is.

Having just left inpatient treatment for the second time in six months, the medication was not working. Paranoia and excruciating fear penetrated a mind still ill at ease. Succumbing to it all, I curled up in a ball on my bed in the uncomfortable stillness of the room I rented in someone else's home. The chaos in my mind was screaming into the deafening silence that surrounded me, while alone in my room. I was abandoned and alone with a disease yet to be controlled. I was trapped in myself, with what appeared to be no way out. Uncontrollable tears began to fall. While drifting in and out of sleep, profound words penetrated my mind.

"Tell them about Me."

Startled, I did what any resident of the natural world would do. I feared and doubted. Raised a Catholic, it was in my spiritual purview to believe that this was a divine appointment and intervention. I was no stranger to the prophetic nature of the Bible, and the true stories of Abraham, Moses and others throughout Biblical history who literally heard the Voice of God. They were prophets and disciples, however. Who was I after all? Why would God choose this wayward, underserving soul who had strayed for so long? It calls to mind the parable that Jesus told in the Gospels of Matthew and Luke.

"If a man owns a hundred sheep, and one of them wanders away, will he not leave the ninety-nine on the hills and go to look for the one that wandered off? —- Matthew 18:12 NIV

I had wandered off, but the Good Shepherd came looking for me.

There was no one else in the room to corroborate this deep experience. Truth be told, if there had been someone else in the room, would they have heard Him? Was it even necessary for anyone else to hear Him? Faith tells me, no. His Voice was loving, and not at all judgmental, though I was filled with self-judgment and self-loathing, and He knew it. He knew all.

Still, I wondered if that Voice was real, or was it a dream? Perhaps it was a little bit of both? We do know that God is able to reveal Himself to people in dreams, as He declared in Acts 2:17.

"...God declares, that I will pour out My Spirit upon all mankind, and your sons and your daughters shall prophesy (*telling forth the divine counsels) and your young men shall see visions (*divinely granted appearances), and your old men shall dream (*divinely suggested) dreams." - Acts 2:17 AMP

Steeped heavily in the human condition however, more questions lingered. *Was I really just chosen to tell people about the Glory of God?* Deep down, there was nothing to question. This was a divine encounter. Jesus met me in my extreme brokenness, and it wouldn't be long before everything began to change, before He would make my paths straight.

Though it was impossible to see at the time through a raging, chronic illness, His intention appeared to be two-fold. First, it was kind of a foreshadowing. Jesus was about to work some huge miracles in my life, and He wanted me to testify to His infinite glory, and He would reveal how to do that in His perfect time.

Secondly, as it became clear years later, He wanted me to forgive all who hurt me, and this was the way He wanted me to do it. *"Tell Them About Me."* In other words, be a light in the darkness. He wanted me to go out and glorify Him with my life. It's the last thing we hear every Sunday as the priest concludes the beautiful Catholic Mass.

Tell Them About Me

The Lord moves in mysterious ways, and this experience remains a beautiful mystery, '*the mystery of faith*' hidden within God, as the Catholic Church proclaims. We are only meant to know what God wants to reveal to us, but because we serve a living God, He can send the Holy Spirit to reach us in subtle and not so subtle ways. What a beautiful gift!

Many living merely in the secular world might never believe or encounter God in this way. It would not be in their frame of reference, so to speak. Believing is a matter of faith, and this was a moment of Divine Mercy, and complete surrender.

Having wondered for so long if God was listening, this is proof that He was. After all, it is we who tune out God, not the other way around. We live in the natural world, but God, through His omnipresence and the power of the Holy Spirit, invites us to walk in the supernatural world with Him.

I kept this experience to myself for years, fearing no one would believe it, but rather, chalk it up to an impaired state of mind. My psychologist did, and I later regretted telling him about it. His disbelief gave me caution for years as to whether to speak about it in public. God was so patient, and He revealed more in time.

Since He hadn't made the next steps clear yet, I simply tried to put Him in the center of everything and lead by example, though often, did so imperfectly. In learning to thank Him for everything that was good, and even not so good, life began to improve exponentially.

"*Rejoice always, pray continually, give thanks in all circumstances; for this is God's will for you in Christ Jesus.*"

— *1 Thessalonians 5:16-18*

Anyone can thank Him and praise Him when things are going their way but thanking God for the valleys and for His lessons within them, that's when the miracles happen. That's when things really changed personally, musically and of course, spiritually. God truly poured Himself into every aspect of a once broken life, and it all began to fall into place. Little by little, He revealed His plan. He used His gift of music to do it, and consequently, I learned to love the Giver much more than His many gifts.

Life has by no means been perfect since this divine encounter. I am by no means perfect. In fact, I am more aware of my sins. It's ironic how true the words of Billy Graham.

"The closer you get to Christ, the more sinful you are going to feel." —- Billy Graham

As life evolved, God straightened those crooked lines, but without good mental health, His will was very hard to do. God is a Healer. He is a patient, loving and merciful Healer, Who was slow to anger when it took years for this stubborn soul to surrender.

When you think about it, that supernatural experience is scripturally sound. Think of Matthew 28.

"Therefore go and make disciples of all nations, baptizing them in the name of the Father and of the son and of the Holy Spirit, and teaching them to obey everything I have commanded you. And surely I am with you always, to the very end of the age."

—-*Matthew 28:19*

In other words, help bring people to faith in Jesus Christ and His Gospel. Help them to know His Divine Mercy, as He commanded. This testimony may even change the heart of an unbeliever or two. Belief is a matter of faith, as with all the miracles we read about in the Bible, like this one.

Then He touched their eyes, saying 'According to your faith, be it unto you…'
-Matthew 9:29 KJV

He did indeed open my eyes. He did so patiently, little by little, bringing me home to the Catholic Church.

***

The Byzantine Melkite Greek Catholic Church, where I was raised, is almost parallel to Greek Orthodox. While the Greek Orthodox Church has its own Patriarch, they do not follow the Pope. The Melkite church has its own Patriarch, but it is also in Communion with Rome. Think of him as kind of the lesser of two equals as compared to our Holy Father.

St. Elias is comprised mostly of Lebanese parishioners. Some are American born like my family, others are directly from Lebanon or have family there whom they frequently visit.

For over fifty years, the order of the priesthood was Basillian Salvatorian, and the priests came directly from Lebanon. The Mass is said predominantly in Arabic, Greek and also some English.

The first priest, Father Ignatius Ghattas, was the reason St. Elias Church was built, and he remained there for nearly forty years. He was *old school*, a true scholar when it came to theology, and he went on to become Bishop Ghattas not long before he died.

He was fully invested in the lives of everyone in his parish. Fond memories flood to mind of him coming to bless our home, as he did with all parish families. He sprinkled holy water and sang prayers into every room. As a child, I eagerly lead him around the house.

Earliest memories of church, however, are as a member of the choir, singing with my dad, sister, and cousins from the time I was about five years old. My Godmother was the choir director. This laid a foundation of deeply rooted faith. It's hard to look back now and remember straying from its elegance for years.

St. Elias has beautifully colorful stained glass windows depicting Biblical scenes like the Dormition of Mary, Jesus with the little children, Daniel in the lion's den and the Ascension of Christ. Then there was the incense, the intoxicating scent of the incense. As the priest would swing the thurible that dangled from chains, the smoke would fill the church with an overpowering scent that would sear itself into our clothing and our hair for the rest of the day. That's how intense it was, and it was indicative of the Divine Liturgy in the Eastern Rite.

Finally, there was the music. Incredible Middle Eastern, minor melodies and harmony became entrenched in my musical DNA throughout my entire childhood and for the rest of my life. It was impossible to avoid getting emotional or to ignore the presence of God, who can and will use everyone and everything to draw His children closer to Him, as future worship experiences would also prove.

***

Returning home to Ohio after more than a decade in LA, proved to be significantly constructive and advantageous. Healthy and thriving musically, it was music that brought me to a Monday night rehearsal in East Cleveland, where a Gospel choir rehearsed within a Protestant church called Faith Church of Glenville. The praise and worship there was so incredibly memorable. It was non-denominational but had a bit of a Pentecostal feel to it.

There was no intoxicating incense or beautiful stain glass windows. In fact, the church and its walls were almost completely barren, but the worship was brimful and overflowing with charismatic voices. It was not uncommon for the congregation to be crying while worshipping and shouting "Jesus! Hallelujah!" with their hands in the air. Some would *fall out* on the floor or even out of nowhere, begin running around the entire church during the pastor's lesson, which was their much longer version of a Catholic homily.

Then there was the soul-stirring Gospel music that had everyone hand clapping and foot-stomping for hours. It was a beautiful culture shock for this Catholic girl. It was a faith experience I'm certain the Lord had sent, even if only temporarily.

The members of the church were all so deeply prayerful and their worship was incredibly moving. Catholics can all learn a lot from this kind of faith expression. It is deep and intense. I'm told there are charismatic Catholic Churches out there but have yet to experience one.

The truth is, finding this faith expression was neither an accident nor a coincidence, and I began to feel at peace when things felt like they were out of my hands. Of course they were, they are in God's hands. He holds the future. Surrendering and giving it all to Him is not always easy, but it was getting easier. Little by little, the faith life which was broken, was now beginning to heal and be put back together anew.

No longer obsessing over a career, and learning to trust God more, I leaned heavily on Jeremiah 29:11.

"For I know the plans I have for you," declares the Lord, "plans to prosper you and not harm you, plans to give you hope and a future." —- Jeremiah 29:11 NIV

Thanks be to God. Isn't that what we all want after all? Hope and a future? God places us where we need to be, when we need to be there, and it's all in His perfect timing and according to His Will. Believe it and know that surrendering is not a one-time affair, it's a daily activity. Sometimes it's an hourly one, or even one that we experience minute by minute.

Faith Church of Glenville was a gift. It was holy, and filled with God's grace, but it clearly was not meant to take the place of the Catholic Church for long.

***

While teaching choir and keyboards at a Catholic school in 2016, a much deeper conversion began to happen. Nearly a thousand young people piled into a huge gymnasium for Mass quarterly at Archbishop Hoban High School. All of those young voices worshipping and singing together was so moving it brought about tears, but they were not tears of sadness. Coming home spiritually was emotional. Early on however, I was trepidatious about taking the position, fearful it would trigger the difficulties from years prior.

I didn't realize how much I missed the Mass until I took that job and thank God I did. It was a profound and faith-filled experience. Through it, God brought me back to the Catholic Church, full time. It was an example of Him showing up once again, but then again, did He ever leave?

Unfortunately, Hoban decided to diminish the choral position and eliminate the keyboard classes in exchange for a heavier drama curriculum. The job became part-time, and they hired someone with a drama degree. It was heartbreaking, but not to worry, God had a plan to place me in a Catholic elementary school the next year, where I would begin a music ministry.

While cantoring and playing piano for the Mass weekly in my new teaching environment, tears again began to fall. Fragile and faithful at the same time, a once closed heart was opening. Coming full circle, I was beginning to use God's gift of music differently. It was not just for entertainment anymore. It was now also a prayerful, straight line to the Holy Spirit, and an opportunity to give the gift back to the Giver.

Prayer was obviously welcome at Catholic schools. Each day began and ended with someone leading it over the loudspeaker. It was healing. Secular work environments were a thing of the past. Now it was time to help bring young people the gift of Jesus, as well as the gift of music. Through it all, scars left by an aggressive disease were healing. That's what mattered.

***

While denominations are man-made, there is holiness, grace and *some* truth throughout all of them, but within Catholicism, is the fullness of truth given to us by Jesus Christ Himself.

I'm not a Biblical scholar, but the following scripture just might prove that He knew the church would ultimately divide.

..And John said, "Master, we saw one casting out devils in thy name; and we forbad him, because he followeth not with us." And Jesus said unto him, Forbid him not: for he that is not against us is for us." -- Luke 9, 49-51 KJV

Jesus can reach out to us wherever we are, but He will not interfere with our free will, the second greatest gift He has given us. As imperfect human beings however, we tend to get in His way and let the noise of this life drown Him out. It can leave a hole in our hearts. Don't be afraid of it. God allows that hole to stay there only until we learn to fill it with Him. That is the beautiful thing behind all trials. God will use them for our good and His glory. He will use them to draw us closer to Him.

***

There's no turning back to a previous life filled with painful memories and illness. God replaced suffering with faith, faith that He will not fail. He will put the right people on those crooked lines and remove the ones who are not meant to be there, even if we do not fully understand why at the time. Trust Him. He will heal you.

The disease is not gone, as the medication taken twice daily indicates. There are just more tools today to keep from giving in; faith and music, faith IN music. The combination is powerful.

It is not easy to write a book that will bear a soul. It's not easy to reveal health struggles, transgressions, deeply personal spiritual experiences and faith struggles. Truth be told, there are nights I wake up in a cold sweat, riddled with anxiety over who might judge or ridicule; who might decide they don't want to collaborate professionally; who might just out and out discriminate, again. Mental health will always have a stigma attached to it, though I hope and pray it is diminishing, and that this book contributes to that.

You may still be asking yourself, "Why would she put all of this in writing?" Well, it's really quite simple. In doing so, I also get to tell you of the Glory of God and His grace and mercy that are beyond our human comprehension. After all, He did say, "Tell them about me."

This book is one way of doing that. You could say it's mental health advocacy and so much more. It is a conversion story, a reconciliation with Catholicism. It is a Christian testimony.

To that end, publishing all of this delicate information would be downright impossible if not for the Holy Spirit, a deep love for the Lord, and all from that which He has delivered me. He is the divine Collaborator with Whom I write this book. If not, the pages would be blank.

Please take that with you as you read. Yes, mine is a story of struggle, but in the end, I've won a battle many people are slowly losing or have already lost. This book is about triumph. Rejoice in the victory, after what amounts to nearly a lifetime of pain, missteps, loss, trial, error, and eventually, learning to do the Will of God. After all,

For as the body without the spirit is dead, so faith without works is dead also.

-- James 2:26. KJV

The more we seek to do the Will of God, the more our works improve. Life today is a great example of this. Everything we do in this life is a test of our faith. I'm not sure who I'm quoting here, but we get no *test*imony, without a *test*.

After years of trying to please the wrong people to keep from being alone, or to get ahead professionally, something had to change. For too long, it was the only thing that mattered. Their opinion was more important than God's opinion. It was the sin of vanity. It was He with whom I needed to cultivate a closer relationship, and the rest would follow. The rest did follow.

This however, is tough to grasp when we are in the middle of the test. Like most people, I did cry out, "Why me Lord?" I see now that He was laying the groundwork for what was to come. Remember Romas 8:28, because it bears repeating.

And we know that all things work together for good to them who love God, to them who are the called according to His purpose.

-- Romans 8:28. KJV

God wants to give us our dreams and the desires of our hearts. Nothing would make Him happier, but as we seek to do His will, so will the desire of our hearts change. Once fully surrendered, life took course in a different direction, one that God was now piloting.

Professional dreams did not include becoming a Christian author and musical artist before that deep personal connection with Jesus, and it is only through Him that this new dream is possible.

"I am the vine; you are the branches. If you remain in Me and I in you, you will bear much fruit. Apart from Me you can do nothing." —- John 15:5 NIV

Internalizing this scripture resulted in much more peace, humility and some patience of my own. God's divine plan far exceeds our limited thoughts and dreams. For this, I am truly grateful, and it's the reason that *Tell Them About Me*, is less about me, and more about Jesus.

Reflection Points: Things you can do

Take a moment now and really think about what you've just read. Does it hit home in any way? Where do you find yourself during your struggle? Maybe you are at a point in your life where you also question where you belong spiritually. That's where I was.

Do you find yourself bouncing between several faith practices, seeking a place where you do not feel alone spiritually? I get it. I know it's painful, but God brought me to a point where I realized the problem was within me, not my surroundings. It hurt, but it brought blessings.

He eventually put beautifully faithful Christians on my path and ultimately gave me very clear direction. He quite literally spoke to me, proving to me He was most certainly listening. Your miracle is not far off. God has a direction for you.

You see, God allowed me to fail on my own, He allowed me to be driven to my knees. Please, do not let this scare you. Think of what the result was. It was a pure and beautiful surrender, allowing Him to finally take control of my life. This was a move I will never regret, and neither will you. When I did this, He blessed me immeasurably, in His Time, and His Way that would bring Him all the Glory. When Glorifying God became my first priority, everything in my life changed.

Spend time now thinking about those questions above. Grab your Jesus Journal and do some writing. When you're finished, take a moment, and make a list of the things in your life for which you are grateful. C'mon, you know there's something, probably many '*somethings.*' Write down the challenges you are also facing at the moment, and what you hope to learn from them. Write down what you hope will have changed in your life once the difficult season has passed.

Finally, take a moment, and think about what God is saying to you right now. I assure you, whether or not His voice was literally audible, as in the days of the Bible, is not really the point of that miracle. Perhaps it was the internal whisper of the Holy Spirit through whom our Heavenly Father spoke. The point is, God will indeed speak to you. Will you know his Voice?

"My sheep hear my voice, and I know them, and they follow me." —- *John 10:27 NIV*

Chapter 7
God's in the Music, The Spiritual Art of Jazz Singing

Predominantly a jazz singer, I have come to feel that something beyond me takes over when singing this music, especially when embarking on an improvisational solo. It's so difficult to put into words, but there is just something about that freedom that is spiritual. It is a deep connection with a great but invisible Presence.

I have never met a jazz musician who has not spoken spiritually of the connection they feel when playing jazz music. Many pioneers of this genre have spoken freely of their own faith and the tremendous inspiration that comes from some kind of spiritual connection. I didn't get it early on in my journey, but today it's clear. For me, it's purely the Holy Spirit that inspires me, and with Whom I connect. It should come as no surprise that I began to feel this beautiful connection when I began to live a full faith life again.

Before then I had been singing jazz professionally for close to thirty years. I had taken many improvisational solos up to that point. They were nice, but that spiritual connection did not begin to develop before years of living life, losing and reclaiming my faith, and learning to put it all into my music, while also learning to love the Giver more than the gift. It truly is a lifelong journey.

I listened and listened for decades, both to instrumentalists and vocalists. Every time I went out to sing, or simply sat practicing at the piano, I would implement what I could with the voice and the ears that I had, even in early stages of development with both. How it all came together however, was not up to me. Believe that. I did the work; God took care of the results. This is evident in so many areas of my life, but especially within my creativity, with emphasis on the making of music. Little by little, God revealed what would inevitably become my voice, a voice that would honor Him. That's fair, right? After all, it all comes from Him.

Does being bipolar also play a role in my creativity? Yes, absolutely. Remember the author I referenced in chapter one, Kay Redfield Jamison. She spoke of how she felt things more deeply as a result of having manic depressive illness. She even dedicated an entire book to artists who were afflicted and how their depression or manic depression affected their art, (*Touched With Fire: Manic Depressive Illness and the Artistic Temperament*). As I said, I too have loved more, felt more pain and joy, and felt it all more intensely. All that intense emotion is present in my music.

One of the albums where this is tremendously evident is my fifth, entitled *Here Comes Winter*. I am proud of all my albums, but *Here Comes Winter* was soul baring, even more than all the others. It was also the album for which I wrote my first Christian song, which was a huge turning point for me as an artist and as a Christian. The way it all came about however, was heartbreaking.

My dear friend, Bobby Jackson, whom you'll remember I met while I was working at WCPN, passed away suddenly. We spent about an hour on the phone the day before he died. It was a Sunday afternoon. We were discussing how I would release the album. At that time, it was a little sketchy. I had only selected a few of the songs for the album. Bobby was sharing his insight about the direction it was going. He listened to me, and I listened to him. We bounced tunes back and forth. I selected some Joni Mitchel material that was all about unrequited love, loss and longing, three things I learned about early in life having lived through romantic heartbreak in my late adolescence. Little did I know back then however, just how much pain I would endure later in life, and how poignant these selections would become.

Here Comes Winter is about winter in your heart. I had begun writing the title track, but did not yet know how to complete the song. At the time, the loss I was singing about was mostly romantic love. Bobby suggested releasing it in the fall of 2014, with winter right around the corner. It was December of 2013 now. He died of a massive heart attack the next day.

We were close friends for more than two decades. Actually, Bobby and I were family, he was like a brother to me. His death crushed and baffled me. He left behind a wife and a beautiful young son whom he prayed to find his whole life. Family was everything to him. I received the news while at work. I was so devastated; I could not finish the day.

I spent the first nine months of 2014 writing and recording *Here Comes Winter*. Following his death, the rest of the music for the album, especially the title track, fell into place. In fact, it kind of wrote itself. It is a song about loss, mostly told from the perspective of the changing seasons. It was very metaphoric. I am proud of it, but this was a horrible way for it to come to fruition. I guess you could say some material just presents itself in the form of life. It was both cathartic and heartbreaking to write, but the Holy Spirit was there every step of the way, inspiring every word, and every melodic and harmonic idea. Simply put, I did not write that album on my own.

Half of the album is original, and I selected the rest of the material according to what spoke to my heart at the time. Much of the heartache and unrequited love I'd experienced in my life came pouring out on *Here Comes Winter*. There was not much scatting, no flashy runs or inflections, just my heart on my sleeve, open for the listener to hear and hopefully feel. For this reason, it was my favorite album to date, and the first one for which I recorded that original Christian song, *My God Is Here*. God truly was there throughout that most difficult time, healing me again and using His gift of music to do it.

I really became a bit of a reclusive writer during the making of *Here Comes Winter*. Though I had written a lot of music prior to it, this was an important album as far as emotional expression was concerned. I was finding out how easy it was to isolate as a writer. Working on that album required more soul searching than the others, as well as the reliving of painful moments in my life.

***

I was growing in a different direction now, withdrawing from people a bit to write more. The good news however, was that I also grew closer and closer to God. It was a new chapter in my life, so to speak.

I was performing less and writing and recording more. In fact, at this time in my life, all I wanted to do was write and record in the studio. I do so love to perform on stage, but the studio will always be my favorite place to express myself as an artist. That's not to say however, that I haven't been blessed with some killer live performances. Many of them took place right in my hometown, far away from LA. I sang and soloed with Damien Sneed, Wynton Marsalis' music director, the Jazz Heritage Orchestra, and The Cleveland Orchestra at Severance Hall. These were not just high-profile gigs, they were fulfilling, prolific and important to my development as an artist.

I wanted so much to perform and record for a living. Instead, I was teaching full-time, but that was also rewarding. I think I learned to love teaching largely because of my own teachers and what they did for me.

***

I've dedicated many hours not only to my own vocal health and jazz singing, but also to teaching my students to develop their own. Growing up, I was a natural but untrained singer who sang in church, in school, and on gigs with my dad, but I didn't study formally until my early twenties.

One of my first teachers, God rest her soul, I worked with at her home studio while I attended Ohio State. Michelle was older and a most experienced singer and teacher. She was an incredible woman. There are simply not enough pages in this book to accurately describe how much she inspired me to get out there and sing. I am still so grateful for her.

Michelle knew just about every jazz tune ever written. If there was one or two she didn't know, you could never prove it by me. Any tune I wanted to do, she knew and she could instantly transpose it into any key on the piano at a moments notice. This made it possible for me to build my repertoire, even above and beyond that to which my father exposed me. We met weekly for a half hour and did so for years. Her own personal repertoire was absolutely huge, and that was before those music apps that we have today. You know the ones; they list just about every jazz standard and the chords. I have one on my phone and iPad. You can even transpose them into your key, something she did in her head. Yes, Michelle was her own music app.

She had me sub for her on gigs, one time at a prestigious club in town. Being as supportive as she was, she went out of her way to stop by early on to kiss my cheek, wish me luck, and to tell the boys in the band they'd better be good to me. She was very protective of her newbies to the jazz scene. We were all like her children, and she was our mother earth. The gig was at the Capital Club, and it was one of my first professional jazz singing gigs in town.

As I explained in a previous chapter, many of the opportunities I had to cut my teeth on jazz singing were sitting in on other singers' gigs. They were unpaid opportunities, but so crucial to my development. They just loved to be instrumental in the development of young, up-and-coming jazz singers, pun intended. There were also plenty of clubs for us to sit in on jam sessions. These were excellent opportunities to go out and learn my craft with some highly competent players, and they are few and far between today for young, developing artists.

Every week, I would learn two new tunes, transpose them into my key, write out the lead sheets by hand, which consisted of chord progressions only, and bring them to the jam sessions. The most popular one was on Tuesday nights at a fancy restaurant. The Hyde Park Grill was home to a wonderful jazz trio of piano, bass and drums. That was the standard instrumentation that I sang with as a budding young vocalist. It wasn't just for singers either. There were plenty of instrumentalists who would come in. It was an awesome listening and networking experience. They all appreciated the fact that I had charts to the tunes I wanted to sing, as some of them were obscure.

Michelle's husband was a trombonist and he wrote beautiful charts, mostly for Michelle. She was generous, and she shared a few with me to get me started. The first one was a favorite song of mine that Nancy Wilson made popular, *"Guess Who I Saw Today?"* It was the forlorn torch ballad of a woman who discovers her husband is having a love affair. When I took the chart to a jam session early on, the piano player said to me, "Now YOU can stay." I was hooked, and *"Guess Who I Saw Today?"* became my very first studio recording. You might be asking yourself,

"What would a nineteen-year-old young lady know about lyrical content like that?"

Well, not only was it a classic song by an iconic singer, but it also had an unrequited love theme to it. Even at that age, I was no stranger to unrequited love. Though unmarried and a lot younger than the woman in that song, I did experience something similar with that old, emotionally abusive boyfriend I mentioned earlier. Watching him fall for and sneak around with a mutual friend pierced my young heart and broke it into pieces, not unlike the experience endured by the woman in that song.

It was a tough reality for a tenderoni such as me. It was also my first experience putting a painful life experience into a song. Did it do a lot for my singing? Yes. Would I wish it on anyone else at that age? No, no I wouldn't. I mean I really would not wish it on anyone, but since life happens, I would say that that kind of pain should, at the very least, be reserved for someone more developed emotionally. Life had a different idea however, and as with *"Here Comes Winter"* years later, material presented itself in the form of life.

***

Vocally, my voice was really starting to grow, and the musicians in town were taking notice. While most jazz opportunities were unpaid, I was being paid to sing in some pop bands. I was obsessed with singing higher and expanding my range. This was back in 1990, just about the time that Mariah Carey was emerging. I was being asked to sing some of her songs now. I loved her singing and so wanted to hit all of those high notes. As I went to my lessons with Michelle, she noticed I was trying to climb higher and higher.

"What are you trying to do?" She would ask.

"I want to get at those whistle tones that Mariah Carey sings." (She was clearly inspired by another idol of mine, Minnie Ripperton).

Michelle just looked at me. She then pointed inside the piano. "You see those strings?"

"Yes," I replied.

"The higher you go on the piano, those strings get thinner and shorter. The same thing happens to your vocal folds when you go high, and you have to be careful not to push up there."

I could not see at the time that I was to be developing my own style. I mimicked the singers I loved when singing pop music. I also was not yet thinking that God had a plan for my voice that did not include whistle tones. I was not yet including Him in my music.

Eventually I learned to sing the music that was meant for me. That happened more and more as I began writing my own songs, and while exploring jazz singing. It's difficult to be an original while singing cover tunes on pop gigs.

We can't be everyone who inspires us along the way. I was not meant to be the next Minnie Ripperton or Mariah Carey, though they both inspired me. I had to learn that while I could expand my range, perhaps I was not meant to expand it quite that much. Besides, the world did not need another Minnie Ripperton or Mariah Carey. They were great in their own right, but the world needs to hear new music from newcomers, not copycat artists. God was blessing me in other musical ways. This I learned as the years went on, and as I let Him in.

***

I was well received wherever I sang, among the audience, and most importantly, among the instrumentalists with whom I worked. That's not to say that I never made rookie mistakes.

I will never forget the time I went to a jam session and called the tune *"Good Morning Heartache,"* a Billie Holiday classic. I guess I didn't know it as well as I thought I did. When I got to the bridge, I began to sing it in cut time (twice as fast essentially) and was off with the trio. Well, a bass player who was also sitting in was less than nurturing. He was an older, seasoned musician, but not the nicest guy in the world. He began yelling the melody to the bridge behind me at the top of his voice.

My goodness, I was like a deer in the headlights. I don't think I had ever been so embarrassed in my life. The look on the faces of all the listeners that night is something I'll never forget. My heart was racing, and I could feel the perspiration dripping down my neck. There was nowhere to run and nowhere to hide.

I wanted to drop the mic and run out the door. Instead, I gathered myself throughout what was left of the bridge, which I had clearly butchered, and somehow managed to finish the song. I think the only thing more painful than being screamed at on the bandstand, was enduring the 'pity clap' I received from the audience when I finished. While I do not condone the way he went about it, I must say I never made that mistake again and sang the song correctly the following week. I guess you could call it musical trauma turned triumph.

This debacle was clearly not the norm. For the most part I was making a great impression on people, but I was not without my own brand of war stories. I guess every artist has them. After all, sitting in and calling tunes that were never rehearsed is baptism by fire, no matter how you look at it. That's what jazz is. We learn the standards of the Great American Songbook. They become our vocabulary, our common language. We all cut our teeth on them. I was taught that a real singer can come in, call their tune, give the key, count it off, and away you go. That's how my father taught me, and Michelle after him.

I took a lot of chances early on. Though I was still a novice, I never hesitated to scat a chorus. Scatting is improvising one's own melody, emulating a horn while singing nonsense syllables instead of lyrics. Historically, scat singing began with Louis Armstrong, but it was Ella

Fitzgerald who was truly known for it, and she was most definitely the singer who made me strive for it all my life. Ella is one of the biggest reasons that I became a jazz vocalist.

I loved the art of improvisation, even then, though I had not yet developed that beautiful spiritual connection. Endings were not rehearsed, so I had to learn to communicate them with the trio with hand gestures and leading vocally. I also had to tell them what kind of introduction, style, and tempo I wanted. These were all things I learned by sitting in. You could call it 'on the job training.'

Upon graduation from Ohio State, I left Columbus to go back home to Cleveland. I was happy to find that there were also places at home where I could sing jazz. I had the joy of working with some of the most tenured players in town. They too knew just about every tune.

I used to sing at the prestigious club, Sammy's in the Flats. You'd have to be a seasoned Cleveland musician to remember Sammy's, as it has been closed for years. It was the place to be for a long time. It's where Mariah Carey had one of her Midwest *break-out* parties.

The band leader was a sax player who also played great piano. His piano jazz voicing was extraordinary, so much so that I was anxious to take a few lessons with him.

Hank played as I sang, and he stressed how important the lyrics were. I was beginning to improvise more and more, and he thought it was crucial for me to have the lyrics in my head simultaneously. He stressed this with instrumentalists as well. He used to tell me:

"Many of them know all the chord changes, but have no idea what the words are. How can you tell a story on your horn if you don't know the lyrics? That goes for singers too."

That really resonated with me. I can't say that my improvisation early on was melodic or harmonic perfection, but I got in and out unscathed for the most part, especially as I learned to keep those lyrics in my head. After all, this usually took place at those jam sessions. They were the perfect environment for taking chances. It was the only way to learn. Nearly forty years later, I think I am finally catching on.

The instrumentalists were usually quite nurturing and applauded any singer who did their homework and made earnest efforts. However, if a singer, young or old, took to the bandstand as if being a star was more important than honoring the tradition of jazz, they were rarely invited back.

***

Michelle wasn't the kind of teacher to talk much about the anatomy of the voice, but she got results. She gave her students what they would understand. I did not get knee deep into pedagogy and vocal technique until I got to LA and studied with a very knowledgeable teacher I mentioned in an earlier chapter.

Kevyn Lettau was masterful when it came to the science of singing. She was painstakingly detailed, and when she gave a vocal example herself, I couldn't help but notice that her vocal production was bell-like.

She gave me verbal explanations as well as visuals of how the voice worked. Since I have always been a visual learner, they really triggered a connection with me. What she stressed the most was how to sing without pressure and tension in the throat. She emphasized singing with what she called a 'united voice', (5) and that came from relaxing the sound supporting mechanism, or diaphragm.

I had never heard it explained quite that way before but I thought it was brilliant. I was able to really grab onto the concept, a concept that she learned from her teachers and mentors. This was hard for me at first because like many singers, pushing from the diaphragm was how I learned. As a result, I could not move my voice as freely as I wanted to and I would often be hoarse after gigs.

When I learned to exercise my voice without pressure, it invariably moved more freely, and this was so important when it came to jazz and pop singing, especially for runs, inflections, and jazz improvisation. This is the most important part of her teaching for me, and not a day goes by without practicing this technique.

As you can imagine, some of my students didn't understand the idea of using less diaphragm. I had to come up with a way of explaining so that they would fully understand. The best way I could get my point across was to compare it to going to the gym. I told them, instead of using a one-hundred-pound weight and lifting it five times, try using a five pound weight and lifting it a hundred times, with the diaphragm as our weight. I stressed less weight and more repetition, isolating the larynx.

I could see the light bulb go off in many of them. This they could understand and subsequently, they became more open to the technique. I should reiterate that without working so closely with Kevyn, I would have never arrived at my own way of describing this method.

***

Teaching privately was the next best thing to ever happen to my vocal technique. I was using my voice to demonstrate all the time, sometimes teaching hour-long lessons back-to-back for hours. The more I talked about it, the better I got at not only explaining, but also understanding. The more I understood, the more I could execute good technique whether teaching in the classroom or performing on stage. Be it on the gig or in the recording studio, I no longer experience hoarseness after lengthy performances or studio sessions.

    Before I knew it, I was regularly singing the material of singers whose tunes I never thought I'd ever be able to cover. There were those Mariah Carey songs, as well as those of Aretha Franklin, Chaka Khan, Janis Joplin. I was memorizing all of their vocal runs and inflections and that truly helped me to develop and expand my vocal range and agility, until I could develop my own.

    I was now writing songs that had me whaling away in the upper part of my range, the money notes as they are referred to in the business. Musicians were beginning to compare me to Teena Marie. I don't know, it was a great compliment, and she was one of my favorites growing up, but she was almost too great for me to compare myself.

    Compliments are always nice, and I can certainly say that I worked hard to develop my voice, but God took care of the results. My gift and my musical increase, comes from Him, and I give Him all the Glory.

***

    I also had the good fortune of being able to work with Roland Wyatt. Roland was the vocal coach of The Manhattan Transfer, Bobby Kimball of Toto, and other singers who were real screamers. He taught them how to do it correctly so that they would not hurt their voices.

He also started and developed the voice clinic at The Ohio State University. In similar fashion to Michelle, Roland didn't get too deep into vocal pedagogy. He knew it backwards and forwards, but did not talk too technical in lessons. He simply told his students what to do, and they achieved results.

Roland was brilliant. I remember calling him on the phone once, seeking guidance for trouble I was having with my voice. I was suffering very bad sinus infections while still having to do gigs and teach. I should tell you that teaching in the classroom can do the most harm to singers' voices. If not careful, it can cause constant hoarseness or worse. I had to monitor myself closely so as not to try to speak over the students. This was difficult as I did not always have a microphone. Many of the clients who seek out vocal clinics, are teachers.

So, I had a lot of hoarseness, and it scared me. I literally got down on my knees every night and begged God to protect my voice and to keep me from getting nodes on my vocal cords. For a while, I was convinced I had them. Roland, after hearing me speak only over the phone, assured me that I did not. I would ask him how he could tell that just from me speaking on the phone.

He simply chuckled and told me, "Honey, it's what I do."

I asked him if I should be inhaling steam. He said no, and instructed me to purchase a cool mist humidifier.

"When there is hoarseness in the throat, it means your vocal folds are swollen. So, you don't want steam, you want a cool mist to shrink the swelling."

He was such a wise man. It was invaluable expertise that I carry with me to this day, and also pass along to my students when they experience hoarseness.

He also encouraged me to eat right, and most especially be sure and eat breakfast every morning. He strongly felt that a healthy body was essential to good vocal health. Another trick I developed, was to put a little eucalyptus in my diffuser to really open up those sinus passages and throat. This was all according to his instruction. Roland was masterful when it came to vocal health.

I had a hard time taking care of my physical body to preserve my mental health. For years I put the proverbial cart before the horse, caring so much more for my singing, and not equating the two. Ironically, learning how to take care of myself, eat right and work out regularly, was not only helping my vocal health, but also my mental health. You see? Singing helps everything. I thank Roland for this. He got through to me. I guess it's reflective of that old adage,

"When the student is ready, the teacher comes."

Years later, I had the opportunity to sing backup for Bobby Kimball of the famous band Toto. I also sang a bit with Janis Siegel, the alto of The Manhattan Transfer, when she was a guest artist at Tri-C, where I was a student for a bit. I needed the credits to renew my teaching license.

Roland was instrumental in helping to improve her vocal health early on in her career. As if my experiences with him weren't enough, when I brought him up to these two former students, they glowed. They told me how much they learned from him and consequently, how he helped their careers and voices. So you see, you don't just have to take my word for it. Roland touched the lives and the throats of many!

I also had the opportunity to have a vocal workshop with Marni Nixon in Los Angeles. Marni was a famous ghost singer in several films. Among others, she sang for Natalie Wood in West Side Story, She had a lot of golden nuggets for vocal training as well, all of which aligned with Kevyn and Roland.

Ninety percent of my development as a vocalist occurred while practicing and being on the gig. I had tremendous teachers in LA, and I was fortunate that there was no real dichotomy among them, just a lot of wonderful information that I keep with me to this day as a vocalist, and as a teacher.

***

LA wasn't all bad. There were many wonderful experiences, God made certain of that. He blessed me in many ways out there, just look at my teachers. I was able to further hone my craft for a while, and I gleaned many memorable experiences for my musical treasure chest.

As for the spiritual journey of jazz singing, it is truly something special to write about. Musically there is the melody, the beautiful chords I love to drown myself in, and the shared communication among the players. It's all so inspiring.

The spiritual journey however, wow! That's almost impossible to completely put into words, sufficient words that is. How do I fully explain the presence of the Holy Spirit in the music that I make, specifically in the art of improvisation?

All I can say is, He is there in the freedom of it all. He is there in the boundaries of it all. Isn't that interesting?

What do I mean by that, boundaries? Well, music is a wide umbrella, with many paths to take. I strongly feel that the Holy Spirit guides me on where to go musically, especially when improvising. He is there in the secular music as well as the Christian, and it is all a deeply spiritual journey. My prayer before every performance is:

"God, let them hear what you've done for me, and let them know this gift could only from You."

After releasing nine secular albums and seventeen singles, only a handful of which were Christian, God finally blessed me with a Christian album. I wrote several of the songs over the years, beginning with *My God is Here*, a jazz ballad. Many of them were of the Gospel and contemporary Christian genre. Then, something beautiful happened.

I began going to Eucharistic Adoration at St. Mary's where I was a musician and singer on the worship team for the Sunday evening, Life Teen Mass. It went from 11am to 6pm every Thursday. I went every week for an hour or so, sitting in the presence of our Lord, and praying for whatever was on my heart.

I do confess to being a worrier. I worried at that time about my parents' health and care. I worried about my work and income which fluctuated every semester I was teaching. I worried about whether my music and book would ever find their way out onto a larger platform, whether I'd ever make my full income with them, rather than having them remaining my side hustles. I prayed for direction and discernment with both, as my limited human view paled in comparison to what I knew our Lord could see and desire for my life.

When I finished praying in the pew, I ended my adoration by going up to the altar and kneeling on the steps leading up to it, right in front of the Monstrance, and I told Jesus,

"Jesus, you know the desire of my heart better than I do. If it be thy will, show me the direction you want me to go, and make it crystal clear for this over thinker. Direct my footsteps like your Word says you will. Not my will, but Thy will."

It was a powerful way to worship, and it brought miracles to my life. Not more than one week after I started doing this, He began giving me more Christian songs. I can barely take credit for them. Sure, I sat at the piano and wrote them musically, but many of the lyrics were a combination of my own, and His. I used so many scriptures within these songs. It was such a beautifully spiritual process.

Yes, He answered, loudly and clearly, and I took note. I continued to go to Eucharistic Adoration every week and gave all that I had to Him. I emptied myself out to Him, and I wrote more to Him in that Jesus Journal I was telling you about.

These things changed my life, and not just musically. I gave it all to Him, every doubt, worry, fear, ailment. Most importantly however, I gave Him my praise, my worship and my unending gratitude. On a scale of one to ten, my faith life went from a ten, to a sixty.

Music is one of His many gifts to me. It is a gift which brings me closer to Him, especially the gift of Christian music. The Lord told me *"Tell Them About Me,"* and after years of thinking about that personal encounter, He finally began to show me how. This is indeed His biggest gift to me, and this is why *"Tell Them About Me,"* is less about me, and more about Jesus.

Reflection Points: Things you can do

This chapter discusses something very important. The spiritual connection that takes over when I sing, is something I hope you encounter in your life, your work or your art. Think about what in your life right now is artistic. It doesn't matter if you make a living at it. More often than not, people with bipolar disorder, or depression, or any other mental illness, are filled with creativity of some kind.

Do you like to write poetry, stories, songs, lyrics? Do you like to illustrate, or paint? Do you play an instrument? Do you love to cook or design? Could you create a blog or start a podcast? Do you simply like to gaze at a beautiful sunset and appreciate God's creation? There are so many ways to put art into your life.

Do you feel like me when you hear or read what Kay Redfield Jamison wrote about in her memoir quote? Do you also feel things more intensely? There's a place for that in your art, and life is art. When we look at it that way, it becomes easier to live, even when life is difficult. Let the Holy Spirit find you in your art.

Are you a teacher? There is an art to teaching. Are you a salesperson? There is an art to selling. You get the idea. Whatever we do in this life, there is an art to it. When I began to let the Holy Spirit into mine, He poured Himself into me, into my music, and that's when I began writing Christian songs. That's what God did for me, but whatever your faith practice is, seek the spiritual connection. Find the Holy Spirit in your art. I promise you, He's there.

God will meet you where you are. He wants to be present in all aspects of your life. I promise you, when you open yourself up to the work of the Holy Spirit, you will never look at your work or at your art the same way again. He is the source of ALL creation, from the very beginning.

"In the beginning God created the heavens and the earth. The earth was without form, and void and darkness was on the face of the deep. And the Spirit of God was hovering over the face of the waters."
- Genesis 1:1-2 ESV

Chapter 8
God's in the Classroom, The Spiritual Art of Teaching

Some of the most gratifying experiences I have had personally, musically and yes, spiritually, have happened with students in the private and general classroom. I truly had to implore God's help to be a patient and empathetic teacher to all my students, especially the problem ones. Whether they were with me for weeks or for years, every single one has left an indelible mark on my heart.

Funny thing, nearly every musician that I know, teaches as well as performs. Even those heavy hitters in LA who were on the road extensively, would return home at some point and teach either privately or on the collegiate level. Most of us had to do something to support ourselves while we were on our musical journey to a performance career either locally or nationally. Very few of us made our living as performers year-round. I myself, wasn't touring at all while I lived in LA, where I eventually found myself teaching in the classroom.

I'll never forget the day I showed up for a voice lesson in LA with Kevyn. I had just had a performance at a ritzy club in Beverly Hills where the crowd was thin at best. I was performing with some pretty heavy hitters. Among them were, George Gaffney on piano, who played with

Sarah Vaughan for over a decade. There was also Earl Palmer on drums, a musician on many of Motown's recordings, and Wilford Middlebrooks on bass. Wilford was the bassist on Ella Fitzgerald's Mack the Knife, Live in Berlin album. I was both tickled to gig with them, and heartbroken there weren't more people in the room to listen.

    I told Kevyn I was so disenchanted with playing to virtually empty rooms. She gave me a reality check when she reminded me that performing was not the only thing she did. She also did a lot of teaching.

    That was sobering. I mean, she had a much bigger career than I did, and she still wanted to teach. This is a woman who has billboards erected in her honor in Japan and the Philippines where she is very well-known. But she, like many other big names in the jazz world, was not on the road all the time, nor did she care to be. So she found her way to teaching.

    My students who followed me online used to ask why I became a teacher. I never knew what to tell them. They didn't understand the life of an independent artist. They didn't understand what an independent artist goes through before they breakthrough, IF they breakthrough, and embark on a full-time career as a performer. So I told them how much I loved teaching young people to love music, and how my *job* is not really a job, because I loved doing it. I mean, most of the time that was true. The truth is, education was a bumpy road too, but as tough as it was to navigate, those bumps didn't eclipse the golden nuggets along the way.

***

Students didn't think of themselves as inspiring or motivating to a teacher. I tried to make them aware of just how important each and every one of them was to me, even the ones who were difficult. In fact, it was the difficult ones who taught me the most. I really got a powerful lesson in humility and patience as a teacher. I had to continually remind myself of how patient God has been with me, and while challenging, that reminder helped me practice the art of patience. Does that mean I walked a perfect road as a teacher? No, not hardly. There were a lot of learning curves, especially where patience and humility were concerned.

My first full-time position as a music educator was in a Kindergarten through eighth grade environment in East Cleveland's inner city. K-8 is a tough environment because there were days I would teach kindergarten, fourth, first and eighth grades all in the same day. I had to wear many hats and be very conscious of where each class was developmentally. It might sound easy because the students are so young, but don't be fooled. Wow, they gave me a run for my money!

Working with all these age groups was a tremendous challenge. The schedule alone was grueling. I drove fifty minutes to and from work, until winter reared its ugly head. Inclement weather indicative of Cleveland, Ohio would have me on the road an extra half hour at least, both ways. I absolutely lived for snow days.

A typical day began with 7:30 am car duty, so yeah, I was up by five am. I taught seven fifty-minute classes per day, with time for one planning period, lunch duty, and a half hour for my own lunch. Fifteen-page lesson plans were due every Monday morning, so you can imagine how much work I did on my own time. I did all of this for a whopping thirty-four thousand dollars a year. I have to say however, the benefits were nice and I used them a lot.

Teaching young children meant unsuccessfully dodging chronic coughing and runny noses. Fellow teachers and I used to joke that we were essentially working in a petri dish. Germs were inescapable and I ended up with an eight-month long sinus infection. It wreaked havoc on my voice, which never got rest. Yes, my first year of teaching was what you might call a *'right of passage.'*

***

A teacher's job is to mold the minds of all children, but the little ones were especially challenging. Kindergarten students for example, are a real trip! I can't tell you how many hysterically funny things they would say. Their adorably young, unpredictable, unfiltered minds really knew no boundaries.

You already know about my alopecia, which resulted in wearing synthetic wigs. I could no longer afford the ones with real hair on a thirty-four thousand dollar a year salary. I neglected to tell you however, that my eyebrows were tattooed. The first day I walked into my kindergarten classroom, I sat them all down in a circle to sing. Out of nowhere, one of them points to me and boldly asks, "Are those really your eyebrows?"

I was stunned. I didn't know what to say. I paused, gulped, and then heard another say, 'Did you put them on with a marker?"

Oh my goodness! I told myself. How do they know? Adults can't even tell.

So, I did the only thing I could do, deny, deny, deny. Unfortunately, they insisted.

"Nuh Uh! Those are fake!"

"Yeah, and that's a wig!" yelled another little darling. You've got to be kidding me, I told myself.

I was trapped, like another deer in the headlights. Luckily for me, they are kindergarteners, and their attention span is about .2 seconds. I quickly started to sing. They forgot all about it. It was a narrow escape.

I was faced with some difficulties I'd never had before in my first year of teaching. Some students were tough to reach but it was so rewarding when I did.

Faced with other difficulties that year, there were times I wanted to quit my job and run away, but something always made me stay. I was physically and verbally assaulted and threatened repeatedly, but I did not like the idea of leaving my first full-time position part way through the year. I felt it was important to finish what I had started. I also knew how disruptive it would be for these young students to lose a teacher in mid-year. While I did continue to pick myself up by the bootstraps when I was feeling defeated, I was just not able to do this on my own. I truly needed God's help. He most certainly had me in a challenging role and it was only by His strength that I didn't run away.

I'm so glad I didn't. While I chose not to return for a second year, I successfully completed my first, and it all pretty much ended on a happy note. Even the difficult students hugged me goodbye as they headed out the door for summer vacation.

As I said, I learned something from all my students. I was once physically assaulted by a fifth grader, and it taught me how to keep cool in a hostile situation. She lunged at me and held on tightly with clenched fists, pushing and pulling on me for close to five minutes. She was so angry. She didn't like the fact that I took something off of her desk. It wasn't even anything significant, a brown paper bag if I remember correctly, but it was distracting her. She wasn't doing her work. The whole room was distracted and unruly for that matter.

    The other children in the room were screaming for her to let go. In that moment, I had to make a split-second decision to either commit assault on a minor, even if in self-defense, or find another way to stop her. I just could not imagine striking a child, especially one that was smaller than me. I chose to talk her off me in a calm, peaceful voice. It was hard, but she eventually got tired and let go. I mean, can you imagine a better lesson in patience and humility? I think not. I really sought God's intercession while it was happening, and I'm grateful to Him for showing me the wisdom to seek Him and keep a cool head in what was to say the least, a challenging situation.

    An even more difficult part of my job was the realization by staff and teachers that one of our first graders was being beaten at home. It wasn't really what any of us had signed up for, but spotting atrocities like this was part of our job. So was the painful experience of watching the school report the alleged abuse to the authorities. None of us wanted to see him removed from his home, only to be returned after a week or two. It was a lose-lose situation for all of us.

    It was difficult to teach a class where that student had obvious and understandable behavioral issues. All his teachers, including me, needed to find some way to show compassion, while keeping him on task. This was in addition to keeping control over the room of twenty plus students at the same time. They didn't address this kind of thing in music education school. It was really baptism by fire for all of us.

We do not all get the same start in life. Some simply start out at a complete deficit, leaving them with near impossible obstacles to overcome at such a young age. It was sobering and heartbreaking to watch, especially knowing there was so little any of us could do about it.

It's not always easy to evaluate if a student has a special need or extenuating circumstances at home. A good and dedicated teacher has to always assume there could be something under the surface that might not be visible at first. This is true especially when there are behavioral issues.

What was also difficult to manage was the fact that I couldn't help it when their issues became my issues. The day I was physically assaulted, I came home in tears. I suppose anyone would. Clearly this student also came from a difficult place. I have peace knowing I was able to show her kindness in that moment rather than violence. Thank God I kept a cool head, but I was visibly shaken afterwards. I just wasn't the type to let things like this roll off of me.

Truth be told, there were many days as a teacher in this, my first professional year, when I came home in tears, but not to the point of clinical depression. I was in remission by now, and that was really the only reason I was able to handle it all. I was stressed out, but I was not episodic. It's important to know the difference. I was strong, but I was also emotional. I wanted to make a difference, but I rarely felt that I could. I never thought I was making an impact on the lives of any of my students, until years later.

For a while after my year long tenure teaching in East Cleveland, I would get phone calls from two, sixth grade girls on whom I apparently did make an impact. They found my website, and consequently my phone number. They were mature about it. They didn't abuse my number. They just liked to call once in a while to check in. I loved hearing from them.

You can imagine how taken aback I was when, after nearly a decade, one of those lovely young ladies found me again. She told me she had been in a terrible accident, and she was temporarily paralyzed. She said she wanted to reach out to me because she knew I would have words of encouragement that she needed to hear.

This touched my heart in ways I cannot even fully write about. You could say I had mixed emotions. I was so saddened to hear of her accident and the trials she would face in her recovery, but I was also so incredibly moved that she would think of reaching out to me. I was tearful when we hung up the phone. They were mixed tears. I was feeling a deep range of emotions that only a well invested teacher could feel. I had my trials on the job, most teachers do, but I was still invested and dedicated. That phone call was proof that teachers often have to wait years before they realize they've made a positive impact. It was a gift.

***

It was following this K-8 music teaching position that I found my way to Archbishop Hoban High School. As I said, I was the choral director and keyboard instructor. I was switching gears. I'd like to talk more in detail about my position there, and why I loved it so.

I had two choirs, one was a little more advanced than the other, The Concert Choir. I loved it but I was so nervous. I started in November of the 2016-17 school year after my predecessor left. The students were used to a different teaching style. If you think it's easy to waltz into a room full of teenagers you've never met before and suddenly teach music, think again!

In addition, I was a long-term substitute, so I was in a difficult position. They were in high school though, and obviously more mature and less unfiltered than my previous K-8 population. Their biggest offense was being on their phones during class. So besides asking them to put them away occasionally, there were virtually no behavioral issues.

The administration gave me a lot of responsibility. I was not to just tread water and do what little I could, which was good because I was not that kind of teacher. The administration really wanted to grow the choral department at the time. They insisted that I take the more advanced concert choir to the OMEA competition, (Ohio Music Educators Association), where choirs would compete for ratings. They had never done this before. It was their first time and mine too. No one really knew what to expect. It was both thrilling and terrifying.

I selected material that I felt was fitting to their skillset. We entered the competition in class B. I did this because it was a smaller choir, sometimes having only one or two students on a particular part. Most class A, and AA choirs had ten to twenty people on each part.

So there we were, competing alongside of some of the biggest and best choirs in the district. Wouldn't you know, they pulled off an excellent rating. They were the little choir that could. The seasoned directors congratulated all of us. They thought it was a great start as their first competition ever. The students really did well. I was proud of them. It was the proverbial feather in their cap and mine.

The details of how things unfolded when I left Hoban are truly an example of how God works. Remember, my position there became a heavier drama curriculum, focusing less on the choir and completely eliminating the keyboard classes. It had been a successful year, but now I was plagued with having no work to look forward to in the coming school year. I was worried, which really went against my faith. After all, we cannot worry and trust God at the same time.

    I knew what I had to do, and I began to pray about it. Then I got a phone call. It was another Catholic school where I had recently submitted a resume. After two brief interviews, I was hired in May, and I found myself teaching K-8th grade music again. God truly provided. Deep down I knew He would. There was really no need to worry.

    My brief tenure at this school however, did not end the way I would have hoped. The principal evaluated one of my junior high lessons on Jazz and Blues for Black History Month. It was about the history of American Music, rooted in Spirituals and Slave Songs, giving way to the Blues. It was a history lesson in addition to a musical one. Cross curriculum lessons were my goal in the general music classroom. She reprimanded me for teaching spirituals to seventh graders, stating they did not have the *prior knowledge* for a lesson like that. I of course disagreed, and didn't hesitate to tell her so.

    The remainder of that year was filled with an awkward, uncomfortable stress between us and it appeared I could do nothing right, despite the wildly successful spring concert I directed and arranged. The parents and students couldn't say enough about how much they enjoyed it. The principal however, said not a word. I was not asked to return the following year.

There I was, looking again at having no job in the coming year. This time, I did not worry. I knew that I had done my best there and that God had something better in store for me. I could not have been more right. I put my trust in God, and wouldn't you know? He provided again. I was hired on as the Adjunct Professor of Applied Vocal Jazz at Kent State University. Talk about switching gears!

Now I was truly in my element. I was teaching twenty-somethings about jazz singing. It was a perfect fit. I was teaching privately as well as co-directing the jazz vocal ensemble with my friend and mentor. Chris became my high school choir director when I was a student at Brooklyn High School. It was his first teaching job. He was twenty-three years old and I was a Sophomore of sixteen. Little did we know that we would have a life-long friendship and ultimately become colleagues.

Following high school, we stayed in touch while I was away at Ohio State, also his Alma Mater. As I said earlier, I was in the Scarlet and Gray Show Choir there, as he was when he attended. We had much in common.

In the Fall of 2009, I was getting my second degree in Music Education at Kent State. Wouldn't you know, he had just completed his Doctorate Degree and was now teaching there. He started the vocal jazz ensemble of which I became part. It was twenty-some years since I was his high school student. We had come full circle, and I was now his college student before later becoming his colleague.

I joined the faculty in the 2018-19 school year. They brought me in just as fall semester was beginning. There was very little time to promote these new voice classes, so the semester began with only five half-hour students. That grew to fourteen in the spring, and my studio continued to grow each semester.

The only downside to being an adjunct professor is that you are paid by the university according to how many students you have. Some semesters I had twenty, some I had seven and everything in between. I recruited heavily but the stress of wondering what my income would be every semester was tough to take. It was worth it however. I loved my life.

Lucky for me I was also utilizing my teaching credential by teaching young people Jazz and Blues to complement my work as an adjunct professor through Open Tone Music. I taught at risk kids in their after school and summer music programs which were conducted at the Boys and Girls Clubs and YMCAs throughout inner Akron and Cleveland communities. I guess you could say that this population was becoming an area of specialty for me.

***

These few years were true evidence that I was living in remission. The stress of transitions like this would have been far more difficult if not. I experienced five career moves in four years, each one a different age population than the one before. Wow, what a roller coaster ride, but I continued to thrive. That would have been impossible had my health not stabilized.

By this time, I was compliant with treatment, and that was paramount in my recovery. Remission did not mean I no longer needed medication. Remission meant finally finding the *right* medication. It took time, but my doctors in Cleveland were wonderful, and God was my healer, healing me through the right treatment, giving me this unique testimony,

I couldn't remember a longer stretch of time that I had lived with no real symptoms. There was nothing interfering with my life, my work or even my sleep. I was however, working full-time now, and life did get a bit stressful at times. It would for anyone.

As I mentioned earlier, I did have what I will refer to now as *'first year teacher tears,'* the emotional result of trying hard to make a difference while hitting some rocky terrain. Again, they were not tears that led to depression, and I knew it. They were more of an emotional release. It's important that people with bipolar disorder know the difference.

I was experiencing emotions that simply came from living a full life with legitimate ups and downs. Tears are not always an indication of illness. Bipolar or not, human beings experience emotions, and I will always be an emotional person. I continue to feel things more deeply. Most people with bipolar disorder do.

Let's face it, tears can be a normal and almost expected part of anyone's life. After all, who wants to go through life emotionless? Why would any artist try to make music without emotion? Why would any teacher teach students, void of any emotion? Even more importantly, why would any Christian pray to God, with no emotion?

I went to God in tears a lot during my first year as a teacher, and I know that He caught and dried every one, giving me the strength to return the next day. Most importantly, He taught me that sometimes in life, there is a healthy place for tears, and that has nothing to do with bipolar disorder.

"You keep track of all my sorrows. You have collected all my tears in your bottle. You have recorded each one in Your book.

Maria Eva Jacobs

——— *Psalm 56:8 NLT*

It is further proof of His Grace and Mercy, and it is another reason why *Tell Them About Me*, is less about me, and more about Jesus.

Reflection Points: Things you can do

Chapter Eight is filled with rich experiences of my life as a teacher, and all the ups and downs that went with it. These career moves mark the first time I began working full-time in years. I went through it in remission, but as I said, not without a full range of emotions, sometimes feeling things deeply enough to be in tears occasionally, but not to the point of depression.

Do you also find yourself in tears at times, but you know you're not depressed? I get it. It's perfectly fine to experience emotion. Emotion is not illness, not even when the emotion is sadness. It's important that people with bipolar disorder understand the difference. To know laughter, is to also know tears. To know comfort, is to also know pain. To know joy, is to also know sadness, and those of us with bipolar disorder, tend to feel it all more deeply. Give yourself permission to do that and know that it doesn't mean you will become episodic.

I'm moved to tears when I pray sometimes, and for this I feel truly grateful. I am grateful that I can get close enough to God to let the tears flow. Sometimes I'm tearful as I thank God for the beauty that is my life today, or as I ask Him for forgiveness. Other times, I'm tearful as I meditate on Jesus' death on the Cross and what it truly means, or as I'm feeling awed by His resurrection and infinite grace and mercy. What I know for certain is that God catches every tear, whether it is in prayer, in stress, in pain, in sorrow or even in joy.

Take a moment now with your Jesus Journal and ask Him to hold you close. Ask Him to reveal to you the kind of emotions He wants you to embrace. If you are a feeling person, who is capable of a wide range of emotions, consider yourself blessed by God and ask Him to bless the emotions you feel when you're alone with Him.

    I love to be moved to tears when I am praying and writing in my Jesus journal. This is one of the areas in my life where I would continue to choose to have bipolar disorder. What better time to feel things more deeply than when I am meditating on Christ?

    If you are an emotional person, embrace this part of you and ask God to help you put your emotions to good use. Every tear we cry, no matter the reason, is a prayer that God hears.

    "You've kept track of my every toss and turn through the sleepless nights, Each tear entered in your ledger, each ache written in Your book."
    —- Psalm 56:8 NIV

Chapter 9
Seventy Times Seven, The Spiritual Art of Forgiveness

Bipolar disorder can weigh so heavily on relationships with friends, colleagues, and even family members. Trying to talk it out in earnest left meager results at best. Some treasured confidants chose to abandon our relationship in the midst of some very difficult times. It was painful to allow those connections to diminish. They were so significant, at least to me. One particular symptom of bipolar disorder was the culprit for many of those *'breakups.'* It's called Hypomania.

Hypomania is similar to mania. While it is not as severe, it can be just as damaging. There was a great deal of time throughout life, even while seemingly functional, when hypomania was prominent. It was responsible for greater episodes that eventually surfaced.

Hypomania produces a lot of *'pressured speech,'* fast, frenetic and unfiltered. There was an urgency to speak every thought that was racing through an already cluttered mind. Comically, one might think of it today as word vomit. Unfortunately, there was nothing comical about the way hypomania destroyed robust relations. Many just could not handle it.

Apologizing all the time and overthinking constantly, mistrust cast a dark shadow over everything and everyone. It chased a lot of people away but also made clear who my real friends were. They were few, but they were true. That said, the people who left caused a lot of pain, insecurity and tears, but all of it ultimately expressed itself musically. God makes beautiful music out of a nasty mess, remember? He is always near.

"The Lord is close to the brokenhearted, and saves the crushed in spirit." — Psalm 34:18 ESV

There were many occasions in LA where medication should have been adjusted, but most of the time, the doctors were not conscientious. On the contrary, they were downright inattentive. They prescribed a drug then disappeared, leaving an already damaged and afflicted young woman to fend for herself.

The Cleveland Clinic was much more responsible than most of the LA doctors when it came time to adjust medication. They didn't simply throw drugs around and then vanish. That said, changes in medication were a regular occurrence for years. With all that instability, people who couldn't handle it slipped away without warning. Eventually it was healing to believe that God has a way of removing people when they no longer belong on the path He is carving out. As tough as it may be at the time, remember that. Maybe it feels like rejection, but in reality, it's redirection.

Hypomania is deceiving. It can be a huge boost. It fuels creativity and it can be very addictive. For a while, I wrote this book, and a lot of music almost as furiously as I spoke. Mania, however, is laden with nothing but fear, paranoia, catastrophic thinking, thoughts of harming yourself, rapid weight loss and sleepless nights. It leaves you completely dysfunctional and ineffective at work, school, and in relationships. I fear more than depression.

It took nearly forty years to be able to discern between hypomania and mania during it all. Ineffective as an employee, it was incumbent to learn the hard way just how to cover up and push down those intrusive thoughts and words that came out of nowhere to sabotage me.

Truth be told, talking a lot is kind of a character trait, for most singers. So being even slightly hypomanic would set off frenetic sentences like a runaway train. It's just one of the ways in which the disease manifested.

It hurt terribly to look back and realize that was the reason people probably left. Wishing that they would understand and just accept my struggles, was a naive hope. It was easier for them to cut and run, and that left a stinging residue of anger and unforgiveness. It all pointed to the area of life with which reconciliation needed to happen. That area was forgiveness.

***

Anger was a knee jerk reaction to emotional pain that was swept under the rug while trying desperately to stabilize. There were the mental health concerns and there were the relationship issues that ensued as a result. The former, made addressing all that was unresolved from past, broken relationships, nearly impossible. Hurt and anger that stemmed from an unmanageable life seemed to loom years after the fact. They disrupted new relationships, both personal and professional, with mistrust and fear that they too would judge, gossip and leave.

Peace was difficult to achieve and that became evident by the trauma responses that would echo amidst new relationships, for fear of also losing them. Over communicating, people pleasing, reliving past trauma's as if they happened yesterday, and hypervigilance was all indicative of a painful past. Subtle things became triggers and caused emotional, downward spirals at certain moments. Yes, there was a lot of emotional work to do for a long time.

It didn't help that much of the time, so many of the people around me were judgmental because of the necessary medication. It was paramount in bringing about a more normal life, even before full remission. Ignorance among many in my life, overflowed for years however, especially in LA. There is much discrimination when it comes to living with bipolar disorder. It is a very isolating disease for those who invariably become very self-focused and even more self-critical.

Anger was like a broken record for what seemed like forever. It was buried deep and it reared its ugly head in situations far from where it originated. It had an awful, mental health effect, typically causing more depression.

Part of the problem was never quite believing that God could remove all that hurt and anger. Passivity is not a prayer option. Believe and have faith that God can do it!

"Therefore I tell you, whatever you ask for in prayer, believe that you have received it, and it will be yours." — Mark 11:24 NIV

Forgiveness is more for the forgiver, rather than for the one to be forgiven. Still, for years it was so hard to let go of the people who left, and the hurtful gossip from so many who just did not understand what bipolar disorder was all about.

"You're not bipolar, you just need to grow up!"

How painful that was to hear, and from someone who was supposedly a close chum.

Taking emotional abuse in exchange for being alone could no longer be an option. As much as it might bring closure to know that these relationships eventually mended, it's just not the case. These people, no matter how much they mattered, were gone for good.

When relationships run their course, and people leave our lives, we must learn to tell ourselves that God hears what is said even when we don't, and He can see it's difficult to do the removing, so He steps in.

To be completely honest, maybe He stepped in for them too. I was after all, a self-admitted handful, clumsily stepping all over myself and into situations where I did not belong, unable to make the needed changes.

It was so textbook of someone living with bipolar disorder, internalizing every little thing someone said, especially if it was remindful of a painful situation. Those feelings, those scars and triggers, were examples of healing yet to be done, and forgiveness yet to be given.

In fairness, some of these people could probably see the hurt, and in many ways, it was difficult for them to watch. After all, what could anyone do? In their defense, they all started out as good listeners. On a good day, even I was able to admit that.

Yes, the hurt was most definitely real, but God wanted me to forgive these people.

"For if you forgive other people when they sin against you, your heavenly Father will also forgive you. But if you do not forgive others their sins, your Father will not forgive your sins."

— Matthew 6:14 NIV

I don't know about you, but I most certainly do want my Father to forgive all sins, and I know that with repentance, He will never reach a threshold and with exhaustion, stop forgiving. So that is how He wants us to forgive others. It's like He told Peter when he asked Jesus how many time he should forgive his brother:

"I tell you, not seven times, but seventy-seven times."

— Matthew 18:22 NIV

There is a significant connection between that scripture from the Gospel of Matthew, and the prophetic book of Daniel, 9:24-27, claiming that it would be seventy times seven, or 490 years til the Messiah would come to reconcile our sins. Yes, the most holy Forgiver of sins, and He wants us to forgive each other.

Then the spiritual light went off. The answer was right there waiting for me within the Holy Catholic Church.

It was the Sacrament of Reconciliation that finally chipped away at the mountain of anger and unforgiveness that kept a repetitive cycle going for years. It's just awful how the things we don't let go of can rob us of the life God has in store. Thank God for Confession, which is scriptural.

In the Gospel of John, when our resurrected Lord showed Himself to the apostles, He gave them permission to forgive, or to not forgive sins. He breathed on them and said:

"Receive the Holy Spirit. If you forgive the sins of any, they are forgiven; if you retain the sins of any, they are retained."
—- *John 20:21-23 ESV*

In the Catholic Church, the priest acts *'in persona Christi'* during our confession. He acts as the physical representations of Jesus Christ so that we can confess our sins directly to Jesus.

It's not that confessing in your heart to God alone is not heard by God, of course it is. And James speaks of simply confessing to and praying for *each another*.

"Therefore confess your sins to each other and pray for each other so that you may be healed. The prayer of a righteous person is powerful and effective." —- *James 5:16 NIV*

It's about what's in your heart and where you are in your faith walk, but there is something so incredibly cleansing and sacred about going to confession. Go for prayers, spiritual counseling, penance, and of course, absolution.

God put it on my heart to go back to confession after nearly thirty years. Thirty years! Wouldn't you know, almost exactly the number of years I had been living with bipolar disorder. In the Sacrament of Reconciliation, I left it all at the foot of the cross and breathed again.

With that, self-forgiveness was possible, and a new cycle began. After all, God wanted me to forgive myself as well. Forgiving myself, led to forgiving others, and before I knew it, the anger did dissipate. As those chains broke, shattered fragments of a broken heart began to mend, and mental health even improved, as a giant weight was lifted.

Surrender is a daily event, and truth be told, it's easy to forget to sometimes. Today, it doesn't take nearly as long to realize what is needed. Cue: the Word of God.

Daily prayer and bible reading are essential. Painful memories and fear do not have to enslave us the way only the enemy would have it. I do not know who I am quoting here, but it is important to remember:

"The enemy knows our name, but calls us by our sin. God knows our sin, but He calls us by our name."

Remember the prophetic words in the book of Isaiah:

"But now thus says the Lord, who created you, O Jacob, and He who formed you, O Israel: 'Fear not, for I have redeemed you; I have called you by your name; You are Mine."

—- *Isaiah 43:1 NASB*

God says *"Do Not Fear"* hundreds of times throughout the Bible. If it bears repeating so often, it's truly worth remembering, especially in those difficult moments when we feel out of control with life's circumstances. I'd like to say I never do, but this book is meant to be honest, not to tell you that everything is perfect. Far from it actually. I still deal with difficulties, like you do, like everyone does. The difference today, is that there is a lifetime of God-saving situations to look back on and remember that our God is the God of the impossible. When we can't do it, know that He can, and give it to Him.

With that kind of surrender, we may not always get what we want, but we will always get what we need. God's perfect plan continues to prove so much better than my own. Knowing this is a reason to testify to His goodness.

It's the reason that *Tell Them About Me*, is less about me, and more about Jesus!

Reflection Points: Things you can do

This is possibly one of the most important chapters of my book, second only to chapter six, *The Crooked Lines That Led Me Back To Faith*, as both are specifically about the way my faith healed me where I was the most broken,

Do you also find yourself in a constant state of anger and unforgiveness? I know that one of the most difficult things to endure when living with bipolar disorder is what it does to our relationships. It's hard on everyone.

Have you ever felt it was used against you? Has anyone ever discriminated against you because you were on medication? Did you ever tell someone about your condition, only to have them prove untrustworthy? Have you ever been hurt by the people closest to you because you have this condition? Finally, have you had a hard time forgiving these people? Forgiving yourself?

I answered yes to all these questions, and I carried that hurt with me for years. I often convinced myself that new people in my life were doing the same things, when in fact they weren't. It was the result of trauma, and it kept me in chains before I learned to forgive them, and to forgive myself.

For me that meant going to confession. In the Catholic Church, that's the Sacrament of Reconciliation. We confess to a confessor, a priest, but as I said in this chapter, you can confess in your heart to God, and He will hear you. You can confess to a *'righteous person'* as spoken of in *James 5:16*. It's about where you are on your faith walk. What's important, is letting it go and giving it to God, giving it all to God.

Take a moment now, in your Jesus Journal, write to Him about the people you need to forgive, and for what you need to forgive them. Don't leave yourself out. If you are anything at all like me, it will make you feel so much lighter. We all play a role in the things that happen to us, a significant role. So relieve your heart of your burdens; put them on the Cross! When we confess our sins, God forgets them, so should we!

"I am He who blots out your transgressions for my own sake, and I will not remember your sins." — Isaiah 43:25 ESV

Chapter 10

"Do Everything in Love," The Spiritual Art of Relationships

The title of this chapter comes from *1 Corinthians 16:14*. God has filled my life with some rich relationships today that I am able to nurture, with people to whom I'm able to give my whole, healthy heart and mind. People with whom I can *"Do everything in Love,"* love of each other and most especially, love for the Lord. I'm able to share my faith with these God loving men and women, whom He sent me just before things were about to get bumpy, back in 2020. How great is His Divine Providence, and how great it is that these people are not just in my life for a season, but for a lifetime.

This is what we must look forward to: a full life without all of the pitfalls we once endured living with bipolar disorder. When treatment and medication are right, we can find a life, a life filled with faith and fulfilling relationships that were impossible to sustain before we were healthy.

***

I've given so much credit to my family who never judged me, beginning with my sister Denise to whom I could not be closer. She held my hand through the toughest times. That said, we could not be more different. While I have been the starving artist and the dreamer, my big sister was quite the opposite.

Denise is a pragmatist. No matter what the circumstances, she forges her way through it all. Unlike me, she's never lost a job in her life. She's the mother of two strong well-adjusted girls. She has an incredible husband with whom she has the time to travel the world. They have a beautiful house on the lake, and their summer weekends are spent on a boat, sailing to romantic dinners on the water. I'm her artist sister who spends most of her reclusive time writing alone in her modest two-bedroom apartment, when not teaching. I do not have the time off nor the funds to travel the world, so I guess you could call me a home body, but I'm a productive home body. We have such different lifestyles.

This is not to say that life was always rosy for her. She lived through a painful divorce and life as a single mom for years. Still, she always did what was needed. She always held her own to manage her kids and her career, neither of which suffered. At this I marveled. Her experiences and how she handled all of the good and the bad, set a great example.

There were times when I just quit functioning. This never happened to Denise. Though I loved my music, there were some low times when I wished I could be more like my big sis. Actually, what I truly wanted was to be more like her, only in the context of my own life and dreams. I wanted to keep my art and lose the difficulties. Eventually this did happen. I became more resilient. I guess you could say she rubbed off on me, but it was a struggle getting there.

Life kept hitting me, and it hit hard. Though Denise never suffered the conditions I had, she was empathetic and always there for me. She was my first best friend. The one I shared a room with growing up; the one I used to laugh with all night when I should have been sleeping. She's the one I went to about boys and the one whose shoulder I would cry on when one of them broke my heart.

Still, we were indeed, so different. Denise always had an active social life. I was much less adjusted while trying hard to manage an aggressive disorder from my late adolescence and through most of my adult life.

Money was never a problem for Denise, she was always successful in the career world. She was also in sales, but much more successful than I was in that field. She is a left brainer; I am a right brainer. I struggled and suffered a lot, but Denise always seemed to float right through no matter what her circumstances.

Growing up, and throughout the onset of my disease, she was my advocate. As I said in an earlier chapter, she was the one to step in when my mom and dad were furious that I had failed all my classes. She did that a lot while I was growing up.

With two older brothers, you can imagine that I was picked on a lot. Sure, they loved me, but they were still big brothers. I have this memory that sticks out in my mind. My brothers went out of town together once and returned with a gift for their little sister. It was a tee-shirt with a picture of a little girl terrorizing a dog, tying cans around its neck. It simply read: "I am a brat!"

It was all in good fun for them, but I was only about seven or eight years old. Oh how I cried. Who was there to pick up the pieces? Denise was. This is just one example that stands out to me, but she was there countless times to run interference between my brothers, my parents and me.

Being the baby of the family, I might have been a little over protected. After all, I was an unexpected pregnancy for my parents. They thought they were through having children, then they got a surprise. Actually, they got two surprises. The doctors told them I was going to be a boy and I would be born on June the first. I guess they weren't as accurate back then. Not only was I born on June the 27th, but I clearly was also not a boy. Lucky for me this thrilled my family. It especially thrilled my sister who, up until 1968, was the only girl alongside of two boys. She was my advocate from that point on.

As a young girl, when I wanted to go away from home for a week on a school camping trip, my parents were overprotective and originally told me no. It was then that Denise would swoop in and convince them to permit me to go.

It all became more and more intense when I was faced with bipolar disorder. Now there was really something to protect and be very concerned about. Even Denise became more and more protective. Before I learned how to manage this disease, everyone was very protective. They watched me carefully for a long time. They were instrumental in seeing that I was taking my medication regularly, something I could not and did not want to do early on.

It was hard on me, feeling like I was never truly independent, though I had a fierce independent streak. Looking back at just how hard things were, I know that I was incredibly fortunate to have a close family network, and I was never alone on the streets somewhere, like many. God saw to that.

My brothers, Mike and Dan, had similar stories to Denise. They too had no physical or mental ailments. They had painful times, but also never let them keep from forging onward. They are successful businessmen with happy marriages and families. They were always firm and secure in all that they did, and they never hesitated to be honest with me about everything, especially when it came to my health. I could always count on them for the truth, as I could my entire immediate family.

My brothers were also a bit overprotective, typically believing that I was pushing myself too hard with my music, when all they really wanted was for me to take care of my health. They made no bones about the fact that if I was without my health, a career could never be rewarding. This was the same feeling that my parents had, but something I usually put to the side to get out and sing as much as I could.

Mike and Dan both loved music and dabbled with the drums a bit, but they never had the desire for a music career. They never went out to gig, like my father and me. They just hid out in the basement blaring their albums and drumming along. I always say, thank God we all liked the pop music they brought home. They exposed me to some great bands that I love to this day, The Average White Band, Wild Cherry, The Steve Miller Band, Journey, and loved to play along. On a side note, they were tickled many years later to find out that I was opening for one of their musical favorites, The Average White Band, at a big concert in Cleveland. What a rush for them that I was moving forward, and they never hesitated to tell me so.

They, along with the rest of my family, were always thrilled with my successes, but kept reiterating what they felt my main focus should be. They were right. So many artists have successful careers but suffer behind the scenes in a stressful and unforgiving business. This was not the life any of us wanted for me.

I truly believe, that had I achieved a big career early on in my life, I would have suffered tremendously, and probably never had grown to the place I am today as an artist or an author. God's Divine Providence is at work in my life, and I'm so grateful He made me wait.

***

Now, about those besties who I've known and loved my entire adult life. Sherry, Molly and I have loved unconditionally for thirty plus years. They are musicians, in fact they are both bass players. I am forever grateful for them.

I met Molly while I was struggling to finish at Ohio State. She went to Ohio Dominican College and graduated while I was struggling to finish at Ohio State. We met in some of the live music watering holes in Columbus. She's a fierce electric bass player and songwriter, who is very sought after.

We worked together a lot and have had countless laughs. There's never been a cross word between us. We have been friends through breakups, deaths in the family, relationships both short lived and lasting, the birth of both of her children and living three thousand miles apart from each other for twelve years. She never judged me or any of the things I went through. We've remained consistent friends.

Sherry and I met in Cleveland. She had just graduated with her master's degree from Cleveland State. I had recently graduated from OSU. I also met her in some of the watering holes where we both gigged in Cleveland. She is an acoustic bass player, author, clinician, mother of two and happily married. We've been through the mill together, but never a cross word between us either.

I will never forget the first time we officially hung out together. It was at a Robert Plant and Jimmy Page concert at Gund Arena. We hawked tickets through someone in the parking lot. Though a jazz and classical bass player, Sherry has always been a closet Rock fan. At the time, I was not. However, I couldn't pass up the chance to hang with my new best friend.

We ended up living in the same apartment complex. We stuck by each other through tears and laughter, marriage and divorce and our many other ups and downs. She was another one who never judged me for any of my high's and lows and she held my hand through many of them.

When I moved to LA, she followed three years later. We gigged together and made even more memories. In fact, it was Sherry who introduced me to Richard Sherman and his family, my only other lifelong friends in LA. We were both trying to make it in the music business in this oversaturated city filled with aspiring musicians. Boy, did we ride a ton of waves. The good thing was, we always had each other's backs.

I don't know where I would have been without these two women in my life. We told each other the truth even when we didn't want to hear it. Isn't that what best friends are for? Other friends have come and gone, but Sherry and Molly are written in stone. We remain each other's soul sisters, confidants, therapists and all around BFF's.

Then in 2020, God filled my life with some devout Christian friends who became like lifelong friends in a short amount of time. He knew the storm that was ahead, and He essentially sent me an umbrella before the rain. They are nothing less than Godsends, and I am beyond grateful for them beyond measure.

So you see, it hasn't just been fair weather friends in my life. I have some real gems who have been and still are in it for the long haul. This further heals my heart.

***

If these devoted people in my life aren't enough to convince you of how blessed I am, allow me then to introduce you to two more best friends, my late mother and father.

Mom and Dad were married just shy of 68 years. Mom passed away April the 29th, 2022 after a very long, brutal battle with dementia. Dad died January 12, 2024, after a very bad fall and subsequent pneumonia. They gave us all an amazing example of what it was to love unconditionally, and to *"Do everything with love" (1 Corinthians 16:14)*. They were the epitome of selflessness, strength and faith. To prove it, let me tell you that they were not thrilled with the fact that I was going to LA. They wanted me close to them where in their minds, they could be certain that I was alright after everything they watched me endure.

Despite that, they never hesitated to assist me whenever I needed it. My brothers and sister did as well. When I had financial trouble in LA, they sent money, even though they preferred I just move home. You see? It was complete selflessness.

Growing up they never denied me extracurriculars like dance and music lessons, and I had plenty of both. I took piano, flute and voice. When my parents realized that I was going to be a flute major at Ohio State, they bought me a top of the line, Yamaha, open hole flute. It was the real deal. My dad researched where the best place was to purchase it, and that was it. My parents did not think twice. This is just one instance where they provided for me, as they did all of their children.

They raised all of us in a safe, wonderful, middle-class household. We were not wealthy by any means, at least not financially, but we also never wanted for anything. All of our needs, and many of our wants, were met. Come to think of it, we actually were wealthy, in the ways that really mattered, including and especially in love and faith.

They worked hard to give their children a life that they never had. They were the children of Lebanese immigrants. They grew up during the Great Depression. My parents and grandparents were not privileged, at least not in the way they raised their children to be. They always made sure we had a better life.

I'm not sure what was harder, going through bipolar disorder, or watching my parents watch me go through bipolar disorder. I will never forget the moment they both realized for the first time how sick I was, and in need of medication. It terrified them. The tears in my father's eyes killed me. We were watching each other suffer and it was brutal. It was the first time I saw my father cry since the passing of his mother many years prior.

My brothers and sister and I were incredibly close to our parents. My sister and I were self-admitted *daddy's girls*.

"My girls are 'blue chippers'. They don't settle for second best," my dad used to say when we began dating boys.

Tell Them About Me

Neither of them hesitated to tell us we were beautiful, smart, funny and talented. We were always told we could do anything if we were willing to work hard. They told this to all of their children. They wanted us all to find partners who believed in us and treated us well. Even in all of my struggles and insecurity, these words helped me never to give up, not on my dreams, and most definitely not on my health. I had a rock solid foundation. I drifted for a while, but they never gave up on me.

***

Neither of my parents went to college. I mean, mom took a couple of classes, but for the most part, they worked right after high school. Mom even had a brief radio tenure, where she won a *'most beautiful speaking voice'* contest. She had a natural gift that she was not allowed to hone or pursue. They needed more money than a radio job could pay, and my grandmother made her take another job. What sacrifices she made. God bless her, I guess she passed some radio voice talent on to her youngest, whom she did allow to pursue her dreams. She gave me a better life than she had.

My dad learned the family business from my grandfather, who was self-employed. He taught my father the business. He was a wholesaler. Grandpa did not have the luxury of a full education. He only went through the ninth grade because they were also poor, and he had to work.

Mom and Dad were both avid readers, as their parents were before them. My paternal grandfather got most of his education from reading the Bible, the newspaper, and from the school of hard knocks. My dad tells us that our grandfather used to have a dictionary beside him when he read the paper. When there was a word he did not know, he instantly looked it up. He knew more than most people who did finish high school and went on to college. He had much wisdom.

Even having skipped higher education, my parents both insisted that their children went to college.

"It's a different world today, " they would say. "A degree is everything."

We all agreed.

My parents put all four of us through college on my dad's earnings, which heavily included music gigs. Mom did not work, she was home with us. Financially, this could not have been easy for them but they did it to provide the best possible life for their children.

"It's not what you make, it's what you spend," dad taught us, like his dad taught him.

"If you make ten dollars, you can't spend nine, that's all."

He made it sound so easy, but we all eventually learned how to manage our money. He led by example. A depression baby, dad wouldn't even throw away a paper clip, and he spent no money unless absolutely necessary.

***

Mom and Dad first caught each other's eye at St. Joseph's Church in Akron. Mom was the organist, and dad, along with several others from St. Elias Church in Cleveland, came to visit. One of the church elders likes to tell the story of how Mom kept looking in his direction and smiling. Only she wasn't smiling at him, she was smiling and making eyes at my dad. How adorable! I just love that story.

They began seeing each other at Lebanese conventions. They were in each other's circles of friends where there was a lot of dancing, talking, laughter and similar faith backgrounds, but they hadn't begun dating yet.

At one Lebanese dance, she was on a date with someone else. Dad's band was playing. While dancing, she told her date she just *'loved this drummer.'* Little did she know just how much.

Crafty as she was, she began hiring dad's band for a dance at her church. Still, they had not started dating, but they knew each other a little better.

Finally, it was in New York, at another convention where they began dating and eventually fell in love. They only dated six months before becoming engaged in March of 1954, and they married the following June. They simply wasted no time. They were the same age, the same nationality, and the same faith. They knew it was right. That was so old school. Things are so different today, right?

Though they dated other people a tiny bit, they were essentially each other's first love. They each went from their parents' homes to the one they made with each other. It was a different world alright. In this regard, my siblings and I were quite different from our parents. We were all on our own for years before marrying. Still, the example they set was something we are all grateful for today. Why wouldn't it be? It was tried and tested for nearly 68 years.

There's just something about an old school marriage like the one my parents had. Watching them over the years was, as I said, a lesson in love and selflessness. Sure, they argued, and they definitely didn't agree on everything, but they never held a grudge, and they absolutely never went to bed angry. This was something I know they learned from their mothers and fathers.

***

Both of my grandfathers died before I was born. Regretfully, I never met either of them. I did, however, know both of my grandmothers and I was close to both of them.

My maternal grandmother, Mary, married a much older man, Louie Silah. She was so young and spirited. My grandfather was not. They differed a great deal and things were rocky at times. Back then however, divorce was out of the question. She always used to joke, "Divorce never, murder, maybe." She said it tongue in cheek, of course.

Mary was my Nana. Despite her marriage to this much older man, her spirit remained young and carefree. It was indelible. I was practically glued to her side as a little girl. She took me everywhere while I was growing up. Like my paternal grandmother Eva, Nana was also one of the strongest women I knew, and so faithful to Jesus, with a true devotion to Mary, the Mother of God. She loved the Lord and she was a devout Catholic.

The grandchildren of immigrants, my siblings and I are second generation, Syrian Lebanese and Armenian, my parents being first generation. My paternal grandmother Eva, came from Zahle, Lebanon. Her husband, Michael, came from Damascus, Syria. He was also half Armenian.

My nana came from Ableh, Lebanon and her husband came from Sahbein. Nana and her siblings didn't have any money, and they struggled tremendously. Thanks to a stateside uncle, they managed to migrate to America for a better life. They were immigrants and they too had a strong work ethic. They were grateful to be in the United States. They refused to speak in Arabic to their children. They were in America now and insisted that they all speak English.

My brothers, sister, cousins and I laugh because we heard just little enough Arabic growing up to have fun butchering the language. We did alright in the choir while singing in church, but in regular conversation, not so much.

When my Nana and her brothers and sisters came to America, they settled in Green Bay, Wisconsin where I spent many summers. They lived right on the Bay. When we visited in the summer, we water skied, boated, swam and ate the best Lebanese food in town.

I have so many cousins in Wisconsin. I often wished we could live there all year round, but I guess summer vacations were just that much more special, since Cleveland was our home.

Oh, the stories my nana and her siblings would all tell, and how they all laughed when they were together. There was a total of five of them who came to America from Lebanon, and they never looked back. Who could blame them? Their conditions in the *old country* were terrible.

Recently, I was made privy to some letters from Nana's older sister, my Aunt Sophie, to their American uncle, who was trying to bring them to the states. She wrote heart wrenching stories of how terrible things were, enough so that she wished she would die. Her younger siblings looked to her for safety, comfort and an existence that would make them feel secure. They did not know where their next meal would come from. They had very little, and they were orphans. Their parents were deceased and so was the uncle who ended up caring for them.

They were alone and as prices rose, they were facing a long winter with nary enough resources to keep safe and warm. They prayed they would be brought to America. As God would have it, an American uncle got permission from the State Department to bring these young orphans to the United States, and they settled in Green Bay.

Nana lived in Wisconsin until she married my grandfather Louie. He took her to Akron, Ohio where my mother was born, but Nana took mom to visit her relatives in Green Bay every summer.

At one point in her young life, Nana took mom to live there for a year or more when she separated from her husband. Mom went to school and made her most coveted first communion in Green Bay. It was their get-away, their safe place. So Mom spent a lot of time growing up with her cousins. Most especially, Aunt Sophie's sons, who were truly like her brothers, especially my Uncle Carl. If the rest of them were like mom's brothers, Uncle Carl was like her twin.

Mom and Uncle Carl laughed to high heavens when they were together. They loved to tell the story of how mom would always wait for him so that they could walk to school together. Uncle Carl frequently made them late. To that end, mom would always yell at him:

"I'll never wait for you again Carl!"

How they laughed for years when they told that story, and how we all cried when Uncle Carl died two days after my mother. I guess mom waited for him one last time, and we just know they walked into eternity together. Doesn't God have a great sense of humor?!

Many of our elders are now deceased. Still, many of my cousins from my mother's side of the family remain in America's Dairyland where so many of my childhood memories are stored, and we all remain in touch.

***

My paternal grandmother is my middle namesake. She was Eva Jacobs, maiden name Hammamey. She and my grandfather, Michael, had seven children, of whom my father was the youngest.

Here's a little-known fact that very few know about me. The Jacobs name did not come from Lebanon. When my paternal grandfather came to the United States, he came with his Arabic last name, Zietkhan. When he landed in this country, they told him his name was too hard to pronounce and spell. He was forced to change it. An avid reader of the Bible, my grandfather took the name Jacob, so his name became Mike Jacob. As the years went on, he added the 'S' to Americanize a bit more.

Eva was simply the greatest example of faith that I have ever encountered. Following a terrible bout with diabetes, she was a double amputee and confined to a wheelchair the entire time I knew her. Despite this, she never had a harsh word for anyone, or anything. When we asked her how she felt, her response was always a simple, "You know honey, it could always be worse." My sweet and tender father echoed her at the end of his life when he was bedridden and unable to move on his own. My parents passed along the strength and faith they received from their parents to all of us. It's actually scriptural. Just read what Paul wrote in his letter to Timothy.

"I am reminded of your sincere faith, which first lived in your grandmother Lois and in your mother Eunice and, I am persuaded, now lives in you also." —— 2 Timothy 1:5 NIV

Yes, it lives now in all of us!

Eva was strong and never without a smile on her face. I think this is where my dad got it from. Sunny, grateful dispositions seemed to run in the family. Dad took us to visit she and her sister, my Great Aunt Annie while they shared a room in a nursing home. They needed round the clock care, but dad and mom made sure they were never alone. We visited all the time, dad even more than us. He always peeked in while on his sales rounds throughout the week, and he took us to see them every weekend. Dad and mom devoted themselves to their elderly parents.

***

I knew all of my paternal aunts and uncles, one of whom was my Godfather, Lloyd Jacobs. Lloyd took his family to live in Santa Monica, CA after leaving the service. When I moved out there, I got to spend a lot of time with him, Aunt Lucy, his wife, and their children. I enjoyed spending time with my cousins in California, whom I never saw much of, growing up in Cleveland.

It was Uncle Lloyd who bought my dad his first drum set. Much like my father with my flute, Uncle Lloyd knew that dad loved to play, so he researched and found the right place to buy one. Like brother, like brother, I guess. Dad was a teenager then, and he did not stop playing until just two weeks before the fall that ultimately took his life. He literally played and sang around town until he was 92.

"Oh Boy!" My dad glowed when Uncle Lloyd unveiled his present one Christmas morning. I could almost see the look on Dad's face and hear his voice the first time Uncle Lloyd told me that story. It was one of many he shared with me.

"Oh Boy!"

It was the expression you could hear dad say throughout his life when something excited him. It was a phrase indicative of his childlike joy when one of his kids did something well, or when he was looking forward to a music job, going to see one of his favorite artists in concert, like Frank Sinatra or Mel Torme, or to a big plate of rigatoni Mom would make for dinner. It was funny how, as a Lebanese man, Dad preferred an Italian meal over Kibbeh or Hummus.

Besides my parents, Uncle Lloyd was a big part of the reason I've always had an allegiance to the Catholic Church. He was a devout Catholic and parishioner of St. Monica's in Santa Monica. We lost him in 2009, but his memory and wisdom are woven into my heart and mind, forever.

***

What an incredibly rich heritage I have and would never trade. I have always known that most people who make it in the entertainment business are typically related to someone with a career in the industry. I am here to tell you, I have never wished for a different family, one that was connected. Mine is a family filled with so many personalities and characters. We laugh together, love together, reminisce and cry together. I treasure all of them and the life we have made.

The only downside of having such a wonderfully large family is the amount of loss we have all endured. We have seen so many cross over, a few even before their time. These beautiful people, and all of my experiences with them, have made me the person I am today. I have a sense of safety and security because I am surrounded by people who will always have my back.

My family, and the experiences they've seen me through, are the reason I have become the artist and the faith-filled woman that I am today. They are a big part of the reason I've won a battle many people have lost.

I'm grateful to God for so many things, but topping the list, would have to be my family. He knew when He formed me in my mother's womb, how much I would need their examples of strength and faith. He knew how much both would help me through all of my earthly difficulties, I know that none of it was an accident, and that God surely makes no mistakes, which is why the following scripture means so much to me.

"For You created my inmost being; You knit me together in my mother's womb. I praise You because I am fearfully and wonderfully made" —-Psalm 139:14-16 NIV

My whole life, struggles and gifts, have become the testimony you are reading. They have all become beautiful blessings from above. That's why *"Tell Them About Me"* is less about me, and more about Jesus.

Reflection Points: Things you can do

It was pure joy to write chapter ten, especially on the heels of the previous chapter where I discussed the painful, severed relationships that hurt my heart, and ultimately led to the need for forgiveness. My life is also blessed with beautiful, lifelong relationships, that I have come to nurture as my health improved. I am so grateful for each and every one of them.

Take a moment now and think about the relationships in your life that you are nurturing, or the ones that you hope to nurture. Who has been in your life consistently, through thick and thin? Who has held your hand when you were at an inevitably low point in your life, as you tried to navigate the rough terrain of living with bipolar disorder, or some other mental illness? Think of what your life might have been like without them.

We all have someone for whom we are grateful. An anonymous poet once said, *'people come into our lives for a reason, a season or a lifetime.'* I used to be angry if they entered my life merely for a reason or a season, rather than for a lifetime. Today however, I am grateful for them as well, even if they weren't meant to stay.

Take out your Jesus journal now and make a list of the people in your life for whom you are, or have been grateful. You'll see, once you take a moment to truly think and write about them, you will realize that you're not alone. Go back as far as your childhood. There are people who have cared about you, and there are people who still care. What's important to note is, there are those for whom we ought to be thanking God, who did place them there for a '*reason.*'

Then, take a moment and thank God for being your Heavenly Father, who is most definitely with you for a lifetime! Did I say a l lifetime? I meant an eternity. His is the eternal relationship for which to always be grateful. He is the One who gave us His Son.

"The Lord Himself goes before you and will be with you; He will never leave you nor forsake you. Do not be afraid; do not be discouraged." —- Deuteronomy 31:8 NIV

Chapter 11
Designed by God, A Life Set To Music

God has blessed me with a musical story, a soundtrack if you will. It began at a very early age when you think about it, having come from a musical family. Music has been at the epicenter of my life since early childhood, thanks to my father. That said, Dad had no industry contacts beyond the Cleveland music scene. Growing up however, I did have a cousin in the record business, and he was very influential when I first began my journey.

Joe Simone was actually married to my first cousin Barbara. The first time he heard me sing in church, he flipped. He had a recording studio in Cleveland at the time. He managed and promoted a popular R&B group, The Dazz Band, all the way to the Grammy Awards ®. He was not just a cousin, but also a true mentor.

Joe was a good guy and he was very attentive to my early strides towards a music career. He was endlessly supportive, introducing me to musicians I would end up working with, and offering his advice and expertise at the drop of a hat. He loved my singing so much, that he brought me into North Coast Studios, a big Cleveland recording studio that he founded, to record a demo as a teenager. In fact, he had my father play drums on all three tracks. It was special, and I almost cry when I think of allowing that tape to somehow disappear. I would so love to have it today.

Joe had quite the presence both on the Cleveland music scene and nationally. He went on to work for Mike Curb of Curb Records in LA and became his North Coast representative. Because his career was going so well on both coasts, he was convinced that he would be the one to guide my career down the appropriate channels when the time was right. He just wanted me to get as much experience as possible first. He wanted me to grow as an artist before entering a stress-filled, unforgiving industry.

As encouraging as Joe was, he was discouraging about my moving to LA. That was my dream once I hit my early twenties and began singing professionally. He knew the business, and as much as he believed in my talent, he knew that it was likely I would become just another number out there. He'd seen it happen too often to a lot of wonderful artists.

I had such dreams of becoming a well-known singer back then, and so did Joe, who wanted to pave the way for me. It was just not to be, apparently. Joe died suddenly and it shocked and saddened all of us, but especially me. I was so close to him at this time. As I said, he was a loving cousin who truly cared about me and my career, for which I was really looking to him for guidance. If I called or stopped by his office unexpectedly, he would literally drop everything and sit and talk with me. You can imagine how devastated I was when he died.

I owe him a debt of gratitude for all his time, attention, and love. I so wish he could have lived to see all that I've accomplished, but then, maybe he knows. Maybe he is smiling.

Tell Them About Me

***

I've touched on a few of the albums I have written and recorded, but there's a lot more to tell you when it comes to the musical life that God gave me.

I actually recorded two albums in my early twenties, but there were no independent artist platforms back in 1989/90. CDs did not replace cassettes until 1991, so they remain hidden away in a drawer of mine.

I already spoke of my first official release, *No Frills*, which I was fortunate enough to record with some of Cleveland's finest. Half of it I sang with a pianist who was probably the most tenured player in town. Skeets and I, along with Lamar, his acoustic bass player, played every Friday and Saturday night in the main lobby of the Renaissance Cleveland Hotel. Singing with these two legends made me the envy of every singer in town. What a high profile, and sweet gig that was. In the heart of downtown Cleveland, the room was highly trafficked by people staying in the hotel, but also by many who would just swing through to have a drink on their way to a ball game.

Skeets was paramount in my development as a budding jazz vocalist. He truly helped me hone my craft by sharing his expertise on the bandstand and in rehearsal. He really took me under his wing. He knew my dad very well, so he thought of himself as not only a musical mentor, but also a father figure on the gig. He warned of the pitfalls that could arise from playing in bars.

I'll never forget, one time he saw me with a glass of wine in my hand on a break. He quietly and simply walked over and took it away from me without warning.

"You have to watch out for that kind of thing. You don't need it," he calmly said. He was protective, and as fiercely independent as I was, I somehow didn't mind. He and Lamar were simply the best in town and I loved working with them.

I asked Skeets to play for me on my debut album. An exquisite player, he added such a touch of class to the whole thing. Just ask anyone who knew him or simply listen for yourself.

The other half of the album I recorded with a well-known jazz trio in town, led by my good friend who is possibly the hardest working pianist in town. Mike and his trio worked together regularly, so they were tight. He had already completed a CD and scored some films. He was instrumental in guiding me through the process. He remains a central figure in Cleveland's music scene, and also a well-known playwright.

No Frills was essentially a high-priced calling card, and my first real aural (hearing) photograph that I took with me as I flew off to LA. The record wasn't a real big seller, but it earned me a lot of credibility, as it showed some top-notch players in LA that I was serious. One of those top-notch players gave me quite the anecdote to tell.

George Gaffney, whom I spoke of in an earlier chapter, was Sarah Vaughan's piano player for more than a decade. He and I worked together a lot in LA. He was a magnificent player and had so much to teach me, which I gladly devoured as a vocalist. My first encounter with him, however, was a bit bleak.

I gave him my CD, *No Frills*, and he listened. He was kind enough to share his thoughts about it. Musically, he was so encouraging about my singing, and my song selection, but was pretty dark about the realities of the business.

"It's a fine CD Maria, really fine. We have to keep recording as jazz musicians, just know that it's leading nowhere for any of us!"

Yikes! That was a bit harsh to take. I still had little girl dreams of becoming a well-known jazz vocalist. I didn't want to hear doom and gloom from George, I looked up to him. I didn't let it stop me though. I would not let my dreams be dashed by anyone.

I continued to share my debut release with practically every musician I met. I took it with me when I went into some famous watering holes, to sing with some of the greatest players in the world. I was sitting in with Jack Sheldon, the voice of Schoolhouse Rock's "I am a Bill," and also Merv Griffin's favorite trumpet player, bandleader and charismatic personality. Tonight Show musician Ross Tompkins was on piano, with Pink Panther Theme composer Plaz Johnson on tenor sax. I wasn't afraid. I handed my new CD to all of them.

I often sat in with them at Chadney's in Burbank, right across the street from NBC. I was continuing the art of jazz singing with some heavy hitters, with whom I continued to hone my craft. For a long time, there were many places in LA for musicians to sit in and jam. Many of them now are closed, including Chadney's and The Money Tree where I also often performed.

The Money Tree was also a familiar watering hole for the same studio musicians who would come in late after their gigs, along with some of the world's most noted character actors. J.A. Preston and Roscoe Brown among others, used to make song requests. J.A. played the judge in A Few Good Men, and his favorite song was *Never Let Me Go*. When I sang their requests, they'd put big bucks in the tip jar. This was good because the Money Tree did not pay much. As musicians, we would affectionately and comically refer to it as the *No* Money Tree. What can I say? It was still a real hang and totally worth it.

Another great location for a jam session was the Sportsman's Lodge in Studio City, but they eventually ended up discontinuing jazz. Most of LA's local jazz scene was diminishing, and there were fewer places for jazz artists to continue to perform.

On a brighter note, I was lucky to move on to places like the Ritz Carlton and the Four Seasons Hotel, who did still have live jazz. At least they were not closing. I was working with even more high profile musicians now. One of them was Octavio Bailly on acoustic bass. Octavio had recorded with Sergio Mendes and Herb Alpert among others. They both came in to the Four Seasons one night while we were both playing.

Sergio was one of my musical heroes. I listened to *Brasil '66* as a teenager over and over again on eight track. Yes, I did say eight track, just to be sure to date myself. What a thrill it was to have gigs like this. They made moving to LA worth the pain and struggle I eventually endured. Early on however, it was a thrill. These experiences amounted to more gems for my musical treasure chest.

***

I wrote the title track to *"No Frills"* while still reeling from a fair amount of unrequited, romantic love. That lyric practically wrote itself. Essentially, it reflected my true heart, which really needed nothing more than another true heart. Significantly reminiscent of that early boyfriend and our short-lived relationship, laden with emotional abuse and trauma, it was my first crack at putting my heart on my sleeve as a songwriter. I was learning to be vulnerable, as I wrote and sang new material.

Ten years after recording *No Frills*, after a lot of living, I started recording *Chasing Dreams*. It took a long time to finish that album. This was the one that originated with Alphonso Johnson and the three tracks he produced.

I was inspired to write the title track following an industry gathering in Los Angeles. Noteworthy producers and songwriters, along with a ton of indie artists, came together to hear each other play and listen to panel discussions on the music business.

My good friends Molly and Kay came in from Ohio to attend, and we had a blast seeing each other for the first time in years. The whole weekend was inspiring but seeing them again made me a little homesick. I had been in LA for six years by now and for the first time, I considered moving home. Thus, the lyrics,

"I never thought six years ago I'd turn around and head for home to start again!"

Well, I didn't leave yet, but I probably should have. In any case, writing this title track was the catalyst for finishing another jazz album. *Chasing Dreams* was completed in Cleveland in 2011. Ironically, the song itself is about coming home.

"So take this lesson straight from me it's not about geography when Chasing Dreams."

The album began with those three songs produced by Alphonso Johnson. Then, I carefully selected the rest of the standards for the album, including four live tunes from my annual concert with Richard Sherman at the Torrance Civic Center. I was thrilled to permanently document this special, yearly occasion.

There was about a ten-year gap between recording the first three songs with Alphonso and finishing the album in 2011. Ironically, I finished the album in Cleveland, but during those ten years, I was inspired to do a lot more writing, much of which fell into the pop and R&B genre's. Most of the songs ended up on what would become my second album, making *Chasing Dreams* my third. I essentially worked on two albums at once, both very different styles. I released this second album, *Free as a Dove*, in 2010. It edged out *Chasing Dreams* for a variety of reasons.

Free As A Dove, did initiate in LA when I met a wonderful guitar player by the name of J Curtis. J co-wrote *Where is the Love* by the Blackeyed Peas. He and Will I. Am sat in a studio one day and didn't come out until the song was finished. It became a big hit for them.

He heard me sing at the birthday party for a mutual, musician friend. The party was essentially a giant jam session. I loved his playing. We spoke, and I told him I would love to play him some of my original music. He came to the house one day, and I pulled out a ratty, tattered, thick, unorganized folder filled with music, including lead sheets scribbled out in pencil, and lyrics with chord symbols written above them. I could not afford a fancy music notation program at the time, so it was essentially a lot of chicken scratch that only I could make sense of. Lucky for me, J did not need to read anything. He could play anything by ear.

I took out my little Cassio keyboard, sang and played, as we went through just about every song I had ever written. One of them was the chorus to the song *Free As A Dove*. He loved it so much; he encouraged me to *"slap some verses on that!"* (J was so hip.)

I'd written that chorus many years prior, back in the early 90's to be exact. I guess my catholic upbringing could not be denied, despite my church conflicts at the time.

The dove is typically seen as an emblem of peace with God, truth and innocence. As a Catholic Christian, I knew that the Holy Spirit showed Himself in the form of a Dove when Jesus was baptized by John the Baptist. Back in the book of Genesis, after the flood, Noah sent out a dove that returned with an olive branch, revealing to him that a time of peace and deliverance had come.

I think this title is a pure example of divine inspiration. I mean, it just fell out of my face. I didn't even have to think about it. I think it was a divine, subliminal perception of something that existed within me. Deep down, I knew I was writing about and feeling the Holy Spirit, who never really left me, even back in the 90's when I wrote it as a wayward soul. God was clearly making Himself known through my music. Sure, I had a hand in it, but God speaks through those who know Him. How does He do it? He sends the Holy Spirit. He was drawing me closer to Him through the gift He gave me. The song, *Free as a Dove,* most definitely has a subtle, Christian undertone, which you'll understand when you note the timeframe within which J and I were working together.

It was during the tumultuous time in LA that I wrote about already. I sought my initial inpatient treatment smack dab in the middle of our professional relationship. Following which, I wrote the verses he encouraged me to write. I was so grateful that I was home and finally sleeping again, and grateful that God was with me through such a horrific time.

"You've blessed my soul, and now I know, how far I've come, to live this dream, how good it seems, don't take me from. Can it be, possibly? I am Free As A Dove."

Once fully written, J took me to Moonlight Studios where we ended up recording that title track, and two others.

The most popular song on the album *Free as a Dove* was *Pour Me A Cup of Yesterday*. I mentioned that this sweet little gem charted and received a fair amount of radio airplay across the country, and it still does. I did not however, tell you how the song came to be.

It was an evening in 2003. I was living with my piano player Richard and his wife Connie, and we were watching television together. It was John Ritter's last sitcom, *Eight Simple Rules*. This was the first episode following his sudden death. The performances of all the actors were so touching, it brought tears to our eyes. The writing was beautiful. There was this incredible line that inspired the song. His wife's mother turned to her daughter and said,

"Oh honey, I'm so sorry. Can I get you anything?"

She replied, "Yesterday would be nice."

That was it. It was such a powerful moment, that I literally jumped up, ran to his piano and wrote everything but the bridge, which took a couple of days.

Pour Me A Cup of Yesterday touches the heart of nearly everyone who hears it. It's about remembering, and longing for...well, yesterday, when life wasn't so heartbreaking. It was a story to which I could definitely relate; to which many could relate I guess, because it is still to this day on the playlists of radio stations across the country.

***

My fourth album, *Art of the Duo*, fell in my lap. I released it in 2013. It originated when my new guitarist in Cleveland called me into the studio to record a simple demo to use for booking gigs. The truth is, I was very pleased with how they came out, and I built the rest of the album around them. They were a collection of duets, several of which were on earlier albums, so it wasn't difficult to produce.

Art of the Duo is a jazz album with no original material, but a lot of original improvisations. I did a lot of scat singing on this one, but my favorite track on the whole album is a simple arrangement I did of the Beatles' I *Will*, from the White Album for just bass and voice. It's my favorite because it exuded a real vulnerability.

***

I was eventually asked to record songs for other musicians who let me include them on my sixth album, *Lucky Girl*. They were my good friend and fellow songwriter Allan Licht, Phillip K. Jones II, and Tommy Coster, with whom the title track to *Lucky Girl* originated.

I really wasn't planning on making another album, but after about two years of recording a single here and there, I found myself with enough tunes to co-produce it with Cleveland's own Grammy Award ® winner, Pete Tokar. I have to say, even though the tracks spanned a couple of different genres, the album had a nice flow to it.

***

Album seven came as a complete shock. I was having lunch with my former guitar player, the investor of the radio promotion for *Pour Me A Cup of Yesterday*.

Jim said to me,

"It's great that you are writing a bunch of new material, but you have a lot of old stuff that's being neglected. How would you feel about doing a compilation album? I'll pay for it."

I really had to pinch myself. I mean you didn't have to ask me twice. It was a great idea and an even better opportunity. The only thing he wanted in return was to be involved in the selection of the songs. So there we were, putting together a double disc's worth of material for album seven, *Hold On Your Heart*. It consisted of Pop, R&B, Smooth and Straight Ahead Jazz songs from my entire recording catalog, plus the new title track.

In 2019, I did the album release party for *Hold On Your Heart* at the famed Bop Stop in Cleveland. I booked some of the finest players I have ever worked with in Cleveland, Rock Wehrmann on piano, Aidan Plank on bass, and Mark Gonder on drums.

At the last minute, I grabbed my little flip camera thinking I might get a clip to post on social media. In fact, the entire first set came out so good, I produced album eight and called it *Bootleggin' at the Bop Stop*. It was not professionally recorded, but Pete did a little tweaking in the studio and I was pleased enough with the recording that I released it through my distributor, to all digital platforms. It was another aural photograph, but one that proved I had gleaned more skills in the vocal jazz genre.

Album nine was a quick follow up, recorded live in the same venue in 2022 and was released in March of 2023. *Back at the Bop Stop*, like the others, received some nice reviews and was even accepted in the highly coveted, Best Jazz Vocal Album category for the 66th annual Grammy Awards® in 2024. While I was not nominated, the academy heard my album, and that made me very happy.

Tell Them About Me

  This album was recorded live professionally, and I had a truly stellar group of musicians, once again, in Rock, Bryan Thomas and Jamey Haddad, when he was not on the road with Paul Simon. How could I not release it?

***

  You've determined by now that I have truly been drawn to jazz singing. I always have and always will love to sing jazz. It's hard to tell sometimes however, what I love more: Jazz singing, or songwriting.

***

  Over the past thirty years, songwriting has become the deep expression of what I could not always express in a basic conversation. Often, I find myself stifled, frozen or detached for lack of what to say when confronted with an emotional subject. These were trauma responses. Whether it be anger, sadness, or an overwhelming feeling of love, I often wished later that I had said more in the moment.

  What I could not express in these situations, I learned to write about in a song. Songwriting for me is not simply for entertainment, it is emotional and spiritual. I write about love, loss, hope and most importantly, faith. Often I write in third person, but the song is really autobiographical, something I find to be a great writing technique that can reach more people, it's more universal. I find poetic license to be an effective writing tool.

  My process is simple. First, I pray that God lead me in the direction He wants the song to go, whether it be secular or sacred. I desire His presence in all that I write. Then, I take pen to paper in my songwriting journal and finally, find my way to the piano where the chords, melody and lyrics begin to intertwine almost simultaneously. More often than not, I need to truly know the story before completing the music.

My songs do not start with the programmed, electronic process. Those enhancements come only after writing the song organically at the piano. Pete, my producer, has always embraced the song's intent with integrity. I cannot even fully express how important it is to have the right producer, if your song is not solely self-produced.

Within my writing process, I never sit down and tell myself, *Ok, today I am going to write an R&B song, and I'm going to make it a ballad.* I have to say, more often than not, once I begin the process of writing, the song tells me where it wants to go. After all, a great melody and lyric can be presented in multiple settings and arrangements. Often, it practically writes itself.

As a songwriter, when I am really tuned into my heart and mind, the song will tell me whether it's going to be a ballad or up tempo, a jazz or pop song. Quite simply, I start the ball rolling, sometimes with a simple chord progression that I stumble upon, then I get out of the way and let the song take over.

Songwriting is not just something I want to do; it's something I have to do. Quite frankly, it has been that way for as long as I can remember, as far back as my early twenties when I first began writing. It was my therapy, and this musical process fills the missing pieces in my heart where speaking falls short.

***

The best thing that could ever happen to me as a budding songwriter was to learn to play the piano. I was one of those kids whose parents wanted her to play the instrument. Even before I began playing the flute in the fourth grade, I took piano lessons at about seven years old. Unfortunately, I was like many that age who just couldn't see the benefit of being able to play. I found myself very bored very quickly. I begged my parents to let me quit. Much to their dismay, they caved and I stopped playing for years.

Eventually, I picked it up again years later, while I began studying jazz voice and singing in the local jazz venues. It was my wish to learn the art of improvisation and scat singing. I knew that in order to do that well, I would have to go back to the piano.

I found a great jazz pianist in town. Johnny was formerly the music director for the Jackie Gleason show. He was a wonderful player and the best part was, he knew just about every tune ever written, by heart. He could also transpose the tunes into any key, on the spot.

It was he who got me playing chords on the piano. As a flute player, I already knew my key signatures, names of notes, and I could read music. Spelling chords was not difficult. Playing them on the other hand, was a different story.

I spent hours laboring over how to turn chords, read lead sheets, and identify different key centers. As a classical flute player, I read everything I played. As a budding jazz pianist, I wasn't reading the melodies, as they were not usually written out. I was reading chord symbols out of these fake books that had hundreds of tunes in them. This was new to me. I would see a *C major 7 chord symbol*, but it wasn't spelled out on the staff. Like all jazz musicians, I had to learn to find the notes and chord voicing on my own. That was jazz playing, and it was what Johnny taught me.

Looking back, I can see that I started the hard way. Johnny didn't teach me simple I-IV-V progressions indicative of your basic twelve bar blues or explain to me that these three chords were the basic chords of Western music. He took me right to seventh chords, ninth chords, and ii-V progressions. He started me on jazz standards, and it took a while to catch on.

Piano playing was paramount in the advancement of my jazz singing and songwriting. I knew that the sooner I could get my hands on the chords and understand how the tunes were constructed harmonically, the sooner I would become proficient at improvising, and I was right. The thing that I did not anticipate was that chord playing would also be the catalyst for songwriting.

When I transcribed a song, (wrote or played it by ear), I could not always find the chord that was played, but I frequently found ones that were pretty, and they triggered melodies of my own. With that, the lyrics were not far behind. Musically, I didn't always know what to name all the chords, so I tried hard to memorize the position of my fingers on the keys. I would hold them there for a long time until I decided what they were called, or at least, what I wanted to call them. I would write them down and take them to my lessons where Johnny would invariably re-name them upon seeing where my hands were on the piano. It took me a while to realize that there could be more than one way to notate a chord.

***

The first song I ever wrote was called *If Only For A While*, a forlorn love ballad. The second one I called *Let's Try Again*, another forlorn love ballad. The third *If I Ever Let You*

Go, and the fourth *She Won't Mind*, both also forlorn love ballads. Hmmmm. Are you seeing a pattern here?

These songs were written not long after my breakup with my second boyfriend. I suppose you could say that art was influenced by life and after all, isn't that what you want from a songwriter? We want to make our listeners feel something. We want to draw off the life we live, a life to which our listeners could relate. At the time, I was living a life in pain. Pain, as I came to realize, was a great catalyst for art, great art if you're lucky. What better way to work out my feelings?

It's impossible to regret the process when you are happy with the product. I am thrilled with the catalog of songs I have written. As I said, I write about love, loss, hope and faith. These were the most significant areas of my life, and they belonged in my music.

***

When I think of some of my earliest songwriting influences, I get how I arrived where I am today as a writer. Let's start with Carole King and her Tapestry album.

Tapestry was an example of a masterful singer/songwriter who knew how to reach her listeners. She too wrote about love, loss, hope and faith, and the choruses to her songs were so hooky. Probably the first to really hit me where I lived was '*It's Too Late.*' This song was about romantic loss, most definitely a universal subject. It was released in 1971. I was only three years old, but it was in regular rotation on the radio for decades. Of course, it helped that my brothers and sister listened to Carole's music and even owned the album, playing it quite a bit at home. I am so grateful that my family exposed me to wonderful music growing up.

It's interesting to know that I gravitated toward this lyric so early in life, before I knew romantic loss for myself. It makes me wonder if it was a form of foreshadowing. Music is powerful, and I can't help but think that maybe I was drawn to this kind of emotion, even before I experienced it first-hand. I was really absorbed in what I felt when I heard songs like this and invariably, sang them with the radio as often as I could. Maybe the law of attraction brought these experiences to me. Maybe the universe was mirroring my heart to me. Or maybe I'm just overthinking it, like most writers do...Ha!

***

Joni Mitchell was another favorite of mine. She was the perfect example of singer/songwriter confluence. Her melodies and lyrics flowed together like rivers; no pun intended. Joni also wrote of love and loss, but much of her music also had a social consciousness.

Her *Court And Spark* album was my first knowledge of her, and from that successful album, came the song '*Help Me.*' Released in 1974, it was the first single and the biggest hit. It was all over the radio. At six years old, and as I grew older, the song remained popular. It was a song about unrequited love. One of the greatest gifts about songwriting is just the ability to touch someone with a heartfelt story. Joni did it beautifully, and because of artists like she and Carole, I hoped to do the same thing.

Another thing that impressed me about Joni, and something else we have in common, was her love for jazz. *Court And Spark* was a jazz-infused record with jazz musicians like Larry Carlton, Joe Sample, Victor Feldman, Jose Feliciano, Tom Scott and more. She could really hang in there with these jazz giants, yet she still delivered a folk and pop vocal performance.

She later proved to be a true jazz singer as well with records like *Shadows and Light* in 1980, also featuring an all-star jazz line up of musicians, and with her *Mingus* album just before that. That was a collaboration with jazz bassist Charles Mingus.

***

Fleetwood Mac's Stevie Nicks is another singer/songwriter who stood out to me in the seventies. Her voice sounded like no other back then, nor does it today. So many young female vocalists sound alike these days, with similar runs and inflections as their popular predecessors. The thing is, no one has ever sounded like Stevie. She is one of pop culture's most distinctive voices. She didn't sound like anyone else.

The album *Rumours* came out in 1977, I was nine years old. The biggest single from that album was *'Dreams'* which I covered many years later with my Pop and R&B band *'4Get The Girl.'* The song was about a break up and subsequent loneliness, which I had a lot of to date. I could truly relate to the song's lyrics.

I knew she had gone through a tough breakup around that time. The song reflected that, making her the kind of feeling artist I hoped to be. I felt her when she sang that lyric. She was singing to him as he was leaving her. It was an emotional story, one that I could have told of a certain someone myself. It resonated with me, and kind of hit me where I once lived.

I did a little research on how that song came to be. I read that she went into a private room in the studio where there was a keyboard. She had a brief break from recording in the room next door. There was also a bed in the room. She said that she sat on it, with her keyboard, and wrote *Dreams* in about ten minutes.

To this, I could also relate. I can't tell you how many songs I wrote while sitting on my bed with my little Casio keyboard across my lap. I also wrote most of *Pour Me A Cup of Yesterday* in about ten or fifteen minutes. It was one of the songs in my catalog that practically wrote itself, and I bet Stevie would say the same of *Dreams*.

She is an emotional storyteller who could really reach her audience, as is Carole King and Joni Mitchell. What's more, they have many years of experience writing songs long before they hit the big time. *Rumours* is Fleetwood Mac's eleventh studio album. It was their biggest, but hardly their first.

Tapestry was Carole King's second studio album, but she had been writing and selling her songs since 1958, first as a staff writer at the Brill Building, and later as a solo artist. She also sold melodies to New York City publishing companies while still in high school. She wrote songs for Bobby Vee, The Beatles, Grand Funk Railroad, James Taylor and Aretha Franklin, to name a few. (9)

Court and Spark was Joni Mitchell's sixth album, but early on as a virtually unknown folk singer, several of her songs were originally done by other, more popular folk singers at the time, which is what ended up getting her signed.

So my heroes, or *SHE*roes if you will, did not come by it easily. They kept at their craft, wrote for others for years in many cases, and quite simply never gave up, though I am certain they were told *No* more times than they care to remember. You can see why they are strong, singer/

songwriter influences of mine. Just listen to those songs for yourself. I wasn't just influenced because of the greatness of their music, but also because of their dedication, perseverance and resilience. What's more, they were women in what will probably always be a male dominated business. Their war stories inspire me, and they make me embrace my own.

I can't tell you how many times I have been let down or turned down because it was transparent who my musical influences were. Whereas for me, that was the whole point, though some LA music people never hesitated to show their indifference or share their criticism.

"You'll never make it with songs like that!"

"Hey honey, no one's listening to Carole King or Joni Mitchell anymore."

Club owners were notorious for comments like that, and whoa! Those were downright fighting words. For me, it has been a gift to have grown up listening to their music, and all of the popular music from the seventies. Much of my songwriting reflects their influence, but that was not enough for God. He gave my writing a whole new dimension, one I could have never predicted.

***

As I began playing and singing in several different churches, people got to know me as a Christian music writer. They incorporated my sacred, original songs into their Mass or service. Early on, as I said, I would have never fancied myself a Christian music artist. Apart from singing in the church choir on Sundays, I just didn't do that kind of material. When I went out to sing, I did mostly jazz, and some pop and R&B songs.

We know however, that God does indeed love to be crafty. Remember, He wants to give us our greatest dreams, but He wants to do this in a way that will bring Him all the Glory. My faith-filled music is truly about being grateful for all that the Lord has done for me. He kept me safe when I could not do it for myself. He brought me out of dark places, revealing to me that He was and is always present. It is only fitting that I give His gift of music back to Him, with the hope that others will also feel inspired. It is only fitting, that I give it back to him in the form of music ministry.

For most of my life, I thought I would only be a jazz singer. Clearly, God had a different plan. It did not unfold however, before a lot of struggles, and not before He quite literally gave me the clear direction that I spoke of in chapter six.

"Tell them about Me."

Yes, more followed that beautiful miracle.

As my Christian music began to evolve, I began blending my jazz background, with my unwavering faith. I call it unwavering for so many reasons. God always provided for me, especially when I found myself wondering where my next meal would come from. My income fluctuated and I didn't always know if I would cover my expenses, but one way or another, I always landed on my feet. That was a pure example of God always showing up.

After years as a jazz vocal professor at Kent State, and a bit of an inconsistent number of students, I ended up complimenting my collegiate teaching career with yet another Catholic school, elementary teaching position. This time however, it was part-time, and it rounded out my teaching life as well as my income. The best part, however, was how it fed my Christian songwriting. I was even more heavily steeped in the Catholic Mass as the cantor and piano player for their weekly Masses.

Playing all this worship music and taking such an active role in the worship experience moved me so much that it really fed my own personal Christian music, until I was able to complete my first full Christian album, *Perfect is Your Will*. It is the musical testimony and counterpart to this written one, and it fills my heart more than any of my secular albums.

***

I have been writing and recording for close to forty years now, living life and experiencing pain, joy, hope, loss, love, and eventually, true faith and gratitude. Those who hear me, know that it is indicative of my authentic self. I don't sing what a label puts in front of me because it fits a formula. God had a much different path in store for me.

My music sells, but I do not make my entire living as a performer. Most independent artists don't, at least not initially, so my advice for those just starting out, put your art first. Life is a marathon so don't try to sprint. Do what you love, and the money will come.

I can't say that all of my songs have been recorded and produced. I have so many lying in folders, finished and unfinished. Some on manuscript paper, some on loose leaf notebook paper. I have so many songwriting journals illustrating the process behind each one. There are lyrics scratched out and rewritten. There are chords above the words, written with no bar lines, such that only I could find my way around them.

Nearly all of them have simple recordings of me singing at the piano on my phone's voice recorder. I email them to myself and store them on my computer and external hard drive. I use them not only to remember how they go years later, but also to upload when I electronically copyright them with the Library of Congress. Wow, I have a fortune spent on copyrights over the years. I can't help it. While some songwriting friends of mine refuse to bother with that, I myself can hardly sleep at night knowing that a song is finished but not registered.

The satisfaction of never allowing the difficulty of the business to eclipse my love for the craft, is invaluable. Knowing where I come from as a writer, and where I am today with a catalog of some, one hundred and fifty songs in multiple genres, makes me euphoric. I've had to learn to realize that; that in itself, is success.

***

For so long I truly believed mine would be one of those artist war stories, where upon rising past my difficulties, my music would break out and I would become a one name artist like those who influenced me. I was such the struggling artist and for a while, at least in my mind, there were so many things pointing in the direction of an antiquated version of *making it*. You know the one, getting signed by a major label and letting them control everything; letting them control you and what kind of music you make. Had that happened, I'd have never created ten albums and many singles that reflect my life story, a life I had to live first; and you most definitely would not be reading this book.

The story I originally wanted to tell, has been told time and time again. It was simply about *making it* in the music business, but God wanted something completely different. He wanted a story that could have a stronger, more powerful and spiritual impact on those that might read and hear it. He wanted to use my story to be a testimony of His glory for others who are struggling with their health, and even their faith.

"Tell Them About Me."

Yes, God was crafting a poignant story of grace, surrender, mercy, and last but not least, forgiveness.

The more I sought His will, the more the desires of my heart would change. Isn't that so God? He never ripped my dream out from under me. He saw how I was clinging to it for years, and He was patient, giving me time to process the changes that were coming. He qualified the called.

Music is only part of my story. Overcoming bipolar disorder? Sure, that's a big part of it as well, but what is the big picture here? It's simple really. We serve a God Who will never forsake us. When we feel lost, He is there. He is there in the hopelessness, turning it into hope; He is there in the heartache, turning it into joy and He is there in the chaos, turning it into peace.

This is yet another reason, another very big reason, why *Tell Them About Me*, is less about me, and more about Jesus!

Reflection Points: Things you can do

    I spent a lot of time giving you a sneak peak into my creative process. I'm glad I did. More importantly however, my hope is that you, the reader, will see the real evolution of music in my life.

    What began as being all about the self, became all about Jesus. What was once all about the gift, became all about the Giver, and it has been so freeing. The ego is real, so it will always be a work in progress.

    I want you to take a moment now and think about what in your life you might be allowing to eclipse God. Music was an idol for me for many years. Can you relate? Today, I want Jesus to be the only thing I cannot live without. It's a hard lesson. Sometimes we don't even realize what our earthly attachments are.

    This would be a great time to take out your Jesus Journal and start slowly. Find a gift that God has given you and give it back to Him. Thank Him for it, and tell Him that you love Him, the Giver, more than that gift, and we all have a gift.

"In His grace, God has given us different gifts for doing certain things well." —- Romans 12:6 NLT

God bless you on your journey.

Epilogue

This book is a Christian testimony about struggle, illness, recovery and remission. Mine is a story which meets where pain and struggle find inspiration…and aspiration. It is a story of gratitude, and an even deeper story of conversion within the Catholic faith. With everything that you've just read, it might be hard to understand. Admittedly, it hasn't been an easy ride by any means, but I am grateful for every hardship that drew me closer to Christ. In weakness, He has made me strong, just like Paul said:

"But He said to me, 'My grace is sufficient for you, for my power is made perfect in weakness.' Therefore I will boast all the more gladly about my weaknesses so that Christ's power may rest on me. That is why, for Christ's sake, I delight in weaknesses, in insults, in hardships, in persecutions, in difficulties. For when I am weak, then I am strong." —- 2 Corinthians 12:9-11 NIV

Bipolar disorder has been a protruding element throughout my entire adult life, but so has Jesus. By the immeasurable grace of God, I've overcome the worst, only to find a richer faith life in the end, a faith which has brought my spirit and my music, back to the Creator. It's tested relationships and made stronger the ones that were meant to last forever.

I am grateful that I no longer think of who's left my life. Rather, who's made an indelible mark on my heart and remained there for a reason, a season, or a lifetime as the anonymous poet once said. I am grateful for them all.

It's hard to let go, but I think it's supposed to be, especially when all of the hurts and joys are wrapped up in the music I live daily, for what I most definitely hope will be a lifetime.

Pain is such a great catalyst for art. I am no stranger to pain, but is anyone? If given the chance to live a life without this condition, I have to say, I would not. I would not trade a thing that I have overcome. I would not trade it because every moment is cataloged somewhere in my life's soundtrack, and more importantly, has brought me closer to God.

God allowed me to walk through this life with bipolar disorder, but look what else He did. He strengthened me and He used every hardship for my good and His glory. It's a difficult lesson, but is there any question that God did make me strong? At my lowest point, He shone His glorious light around me and gave me a very clear direction. He showed me how to testify to His infinite glory.

"Tell them about Me."

Your miracles abound, Lord! I will glorify you with my life.

THE END

Notes

(2. 3. 4.) American Psychiatric Association (2000). Diagnostic and statistical manual of mental disorders (4th ed., Text Revision). Washington, DC: Author 5. American Psychiatric Associatation, (2013). Diagnostic and Statistical Manual of Mental Disorders (5th ed)

(5) Freedom of Natural Voice Production, © 2006, Kevyn Lettau, www.kevynlettau.com

(9)Carole King, A Natural Woman, a memoir. Grand Central Publishing, a division of Hatchette Book Group © 2012 by Eugenius, LLC

About the Author

Maria Jacobs is American born of Syrian Lebanese and Armenian descent. Born and raised in Cleveland, Ohio she grew up in a musical family, getting her start singing with her father, a drummer and singer, and in The Byzantine Melkite Greek Catholic Church where she was raised. Her music ministry now extends to the Roman Catholic Church where she also leads worship.

Today, Maria is a national jazz and Christian recording artist as well as a national voice over artist. She has released 10 solo albums, and 17 singles and written over 150 songs. Her ninth album was accepted for Grammy review in the Best Jazz Vocal Album category in 2024, and her 10th album is her first full Christian album which debuted in the top 10 on the Christian radio charts. She is a royalty earning member of ASCAP and has opened for major acts, including jazz greats Chuck Mangione and Bob Dorough; R&B group the Average White Band and British soul band Loose

Ends.

She sang and recorded with some of the music industry's finest during her tenure in Los Angeles, CA, as well as in her home town of Cleveland, OH when she returned.

You will find Maria on IMDb as a theme song composer and actress for two independent films, and her music is available on all digital streaming platforms.

In addition to her performing career, Maria is an educator who holds two Bachelor of Arts Degrees. One is from Ohio State University in Journalism, and the other is from Kent State University in Music Education, with a minor in Education. She graduated Cum Laude from Kent State and went on to become the vocal jazz professor there.

As a licensed Music educator, Maria has taught music to grade levels pre-K through 12th grade throughout her extensive career. She is currently the music instructor at St. Joseph Randolph and also for Open Tone Music where she works with at risk students and students with special needs throughout inner Akron and Cleveland communities.

Her book entitled "Tell Them About Me-" A Journey Through Bipolar disorder and the Faith Walk into Remission, is her literary debut, but she is also published on some prominent mental health online platforms, including that of the National Alliance on Mental Illness, (NAMI) and the International Bipolar disorder Foundation (IBDF). She continues to speak and do advocacy in the mental health field, sharing her hope-filled story to help others.

For more information on Maria's music and book, you can visit www.mariajacobs.com.

www.ingramcontent.com/pod-product-compliance
Lightning Source LLC
Chambersburg PA
CBHW060947050426
42337CB00052B/1630